Hamlyn

John Pinsent

Myths & Legends of
Ancient
Greece

Illustrated by Jan Parker

Hamlyn · London
Sun Books · Melbourne

FOREWORD

Greek myths can be retold in a number of different ways. They can be explained and discussed as they are by scholars, and this style is employed in the introduction to each section in this book. They can be modernised, as they were by Charles Kingsley and Nathaniel Hawthorne in Victorian times, and by various authors since then. In this style the motivation is made acceptable to contemporary ways of thinking: the Greeks appear as Victorian undergraduates or modern schoolboys. But this type of retelling emasculates the myths: Greek culture is 'desperately foreign' and Greek mythology can only be understood in its own terms. It is for this reason that I have employed a simple and archaic style that owes something to the Authorised Version of the Bible and something to the formulaic style of Homer and subsequent Greek literature. It is meant to present the myths as they might have appeared to an educated Greek of the second or third century A.D., whose sceptical education was not sufficient to rob him of all faith in the truth of the myths about his gods.

Published by The Hamlyn Publishing Group Limited
London · New York · Sydney · Toronto
Hamlyn House, Feltham, Middlesex, England
In association with Sun Books Pty Ltd Melbourne

Copyright © The Hamlyn Publishing Group Limited 1969

SBN 600001288
Phototypeset by Filmtype Services, Scarborough
Colour separations by Schwitter Limited, Zurich
Printed in England by Sir Joseph Causton & Sons Limited

CONTENTS

Introduction

From the time of Homer (perhaps eighth century B.C.) to that of Nonnus (fifth century A.D.) the Greeks told and re-told hundreds of stories about their gods and heroes. From that of Catullus (first century B.C.) to that of Claudian (fifth century A.D.) the Romans told the same stories, giving the gods and some of the heroes the Latin equivalents of their names, as Jupiter for Zeus and Hercules for Heracles. Later European writers have assumed in their readers a knowledge of these stories, and have made use of them, retold them, and alluded to them, most often in their Latin form. Artists too, especially from the Renaissance, have found in Greek mythology a fruitful source of inspiration, and have illustrated the stories, as has the artist of this book, in their own personal style.

This book gives a direct and straightforward account of as many myths as possible, keeping to the genealogical arrangement originally made by the Greeks themselves. Each section is preceded by a brief introduction, which tries to show why they were told in that particular way. These introductions are illustrated from Greek objects which depict some of the myths.

Over such a long period of telling and re-telling, many different versions of the same story are found. Those given here are those which best display the logic of the myth, and some gaps have been filled in. These are not always the oldest versions. The great Greek writers, Homer, Pindar and the Athenian dramatists, Aeschylus, Sophocles and Euripides, often altered the stories to suit their own purposes. The scholars and poets of Alexandria in Egypt (from the third century B.C.) and later antiquarians often preserve older local versions. It was from those Alexandrian writers that the Roman poets took their material.

In fact there are many different kinds of myths and they can be explained in many different ways. Some are creation myths and tell how the world and some of its elements came to be. Others give an origin of some ritual or ceremonial. Many contain what are called *Märchen*, elements found in myth and fairy and folk tales from all over the world: they seem to be decayed myths of universal psychological appeal. For all myths reflected the organization of the society in which they were

4

The young Apollo.
Fifth-century Attic bronze.

Athena and her owl. Athenian coin, 479 B.C.

told, and satisfied the psychological needs of their hearers. Sometimes they preserved traces of an earlier state of affairs.

All the Greeks worshipped the same gods. They came to Greece with the patriarchal family of gods and goddesses which is familiar to us from many other places, e.g. the Norse sagas. They came to a land where local mother-goddesses with youthful consorts seem to have been more familiar, and the richness of Greek mythology arises in part from the interaction of these two religions.

The family of the gods is seen at its best in Homer. It suited a society of fighting men governed by the approval of their peers, what anthropologists call a 'shame culture'. The intense but rapidly changing emotions of the heroes were easily projected on to a supernatural world of interfering gods and goddesses who continually helped their favourites. The classical world of fifth-century Athens had learnt the meaning of guilt: the gods of tragedy are powerful, distant, jealous and capricious. They intervene only to punish mortals who have presumed to usurp the divine privileges.

Greek cosmogony

Greek stories about the creation of the world are set in the framework of a series of mythological genealogies, starting with Chaos and ending with Zeus, high god of the Greeks and 'father of gods and men'. This account first appears in the *Theogony* – 'the birth of the gods' – attributed to Hesiod and written about 725 B.C. It is not originally Greek – those creation myths have been lost if they ever existed – but is based on the Babylonian creation myth, probably as that was modified by the Hittites, a northern people who dominated Asia Minor during the second millennium B.C. But the whole story has been recast to accord with Greek modes of thought. Common to all versions is a number of divine generations who supplant one another until the reigning god – Zeus in Greece, Marduk in Babylon – triumphs. In each generation son over-throws father, often brutally, although in the Greek myth the details are blurred where Zeus is concerned. These generations partly reflect religious history: the old gods are overthrown. It was psychologically hard for the Greeks, who were strongly patriarchal, to accept myths in which son superseded father unless the conflict was thrown back into an earlier generation.

Pegasus. Corinthian coin of the sixth century.

Lion's head on an early sixth-century coin, probably from Smyrna.

In Babylon, the original pair were Apsû, god of the fresh water, and Tiâmat, goddess of the sea. Tiâmat is eventually sundered in the fourth generation by Marduk and the heavens open between the waters above and those beneath the earth. This seems to be the origin of Chaos, the gap. There are traces of this role of the sea mother in some Greek myths, but her place is usually taken by Gaia, the earth, whom Heaven only covers at night. These creation myths are clearly envisaged in terms of Father and Mother as seen by the child. Such psychological overtones are particularly strong in the myth of Cronus and Uranus. There is a peculiar ambiguity in the fact that Earth encourages her children to overthrow the tyrant father and then when they have done so brings forth monsters against them. The Babylonian myth seems to have been re-enacted each New Year by the reigning king: it is not the ritual but the psychological overtones which account for the powerful impact that the Greek myth has always had on the mind of Western man.

Zeus and Typhon. Shield relief from Olympia.

The birth of the 'bearded' Aphrodite. Seventh-century terracotta from Perachora.

How the world was made

First Chaos was born, and then earth with broad breast, and then misty Tartarus that lies under the Earth, and Love, fairest of the immortal gods, who alone could inspire creation. From Chaos, Erebus was born, the Darkness under the earth, and Night. From Night, Day and Ether, the bright upper air where the gods live: she bore them in love to Erebus. Earth first bore her consort Uranus, the starry heaven, to cover her, and the mountains and the nymphs who dwell in them; and Pontus, the unharvested sea. All these she bore of herself, but then she bedded with Heaven and bore the Titans, the elder gods. First Ocean, the great stream that encircles the world and holds it. He is the source of all things, wedded to his sister Tethys the sea goddess. But now he is sundered from her. Then Earth bore Coeus the father of Leto, and Crius, and Hyperion, the sun who goes over heaven, and Iapetus or Japhet, father of Prometheus, and Theia and Rhea, mother of the gods, and Themis, 'justice', and Mnemosyne, 'memory', mother of the Muses, and Phoebe the moon.

How Cronus overthrew Uranus

Last of all Earth bore Cronus, the youngest son destined to inherit the kingdom for a while. For Uranus hated his children, and would not let them come to birth, and they remained hidden in the earth. There were eighteen of these, and twelve were Titans. Gaia made a sickle of the grey adamant, creating that new metal in herself, and called upon her children to take vengeance on their lewd father, to overthrow him and emerge into the light. Only Cronus had the courage. He took the sickle and lay beneath the bed, and when night came and huge Uranus returned and lay upon the earth, Cronus reached out his left hand and siezed his father, and with the right hand he unmanned him with the sickle, as a man cuts down the corn in its season. With averted eyes he cast aside the parts, flinging them into the sea. From the bloody foam a sweet goddess was born, Aphrodite, goddess of love, and she came to shore in Cythera, or it may be Cyprus, and flowers bloomed under her feet. Then Cronus released his brothers and sisters, and took Rhea to his wife, and ruled over the Titans. But Uranus was sundered for ever from Earth.

Birth and triumph of Zeus

Cronus in his turn feared to be supplanted by his children, and one by one as they were born he swallowed them, Hestia the Hearth, Demeter the Corn Mother, Hera the Lady, Hades and Poseidon. But when Zeus was to be born, father of gods and men, Rhea took counsel of her parents, Uranus and Gaia, and they sent her to Crete, and Earth received the new-born child in a holy cave below the forests of Mount Aegeum. Rhea took a stone, wrapped it in swaddling clothes, and gave it to Cronus, and he swallowed it.

But the infant Zeus was nursed by the Ash-nymph Adrasteia and fed on honey, and given milk by the goat Amalthea: his cradle hung in a tree 'neighter in heaven nor in earth nor in the sea', and the Young Men, the Curetes, clashed their arms and drowned his cries so that his father might not hear, and destroy him. Swiftly he grew to manhood, and with Earth's help he overthrew Cronus, and gave him a medicine of mustard and salt, and he vomited up first the stone and then his children. Zeus set the stone at the navel of earth in token of his victory. Two eagles flew, one from the East and one from the West, and there they met at Delphi.

Zeus and the Titans

Then Zeus and the younger gods fought the Titans on the plains of Thessaly for the possession of Olympus. He could not win until Earth told him of the magic Helpers needed in any great enterprise. Then Zeus set free the Hundred Handers, Earth's children by Uranus. Cronus had not released them, and so, each hurling a hundred rocks, they routed the Titans for Zeus and chased them to Tartarus where they held them fast. Then Earth was shocked by the harsh punishment that Zeus laid upon her children and repented that she had helped him.

She bore a youngest son, Typhon the monstrous serpent man, who fought with Zeus in Asia. Zeus took the adamant sickle Cronus had used, but Typhon wrested it from him, and with it cut out the sinews from Zeus's limbs, and hid them in a cave guarded by his serpent daughter. Hermes stole them back, and returned his hardy manhood to Zeus. Then Zeus blasted Typhon with the thunderbolt forged for him by the Cyclops, magic smiths with a patch on one eye, and he pinned him under Etna where he breathes out fiery lava and shakes the earth in his torments.

The gods of the Greeks

The Greek creation myths seem to be derived from Babylon. But the family of the gods ruled over by the sky god is typical of the northern peoples who moved into Europe, Asia Minor, and India at the beginning of the second millennium. The oldest son shares the paternal inheritance with his brothers, and he and his wife rule over an extended family comprising them and his own children. But this simple pattern is obscured in Greek mythology because the goddesses have been identified with those already existing in the land of Greece. Each large city seems to have given her its own title, and some of the younger gods seem to have been originally their sons and consorts though their paternity has been attributed to Zeus.

There are traces of Zeus's original consort in Dione, the mother of Aphrodite in Homer. But his regular wife is Hera, the Lady, a title of the mother-goddess especially at Argos. Only one member of the divine family is their child, and that is Ares, a Thracian god of war addicted to chariots and man-eating mares. Athena is, from her name, the Athenian

The gods on Olympus. From left to right: Hebe, Hermes, Athena, Zeus, Ganymede, Hera, Aphrodite and Ares. From a fifth-century vase.

mother-goddess transformed into the virgin warrior daughter of Zeus and given a miraculous birth without a mother. Demeter is shown by her name to be Earth Mother, and Poseidon to have been only her husband. He has taken the place of Oceanus the Earth Shaker, but retains from his earlier role an association with horses as she with mares. But the father of Demeter's daughter is Zeus, and the Corn Maiden Kore is given by Zeus as bride to his other brother Hades, god of the Underworld.

Zeus is also father of Apollo and Artemis: Apollo is a mixture of many gods, but chiefly a prophetic archer: Artemis is mistress of wild beasts but now a virgin. Their mother Leto is an old goddess, and Hermes's mother Maia is another, but again his father is Zeus: a god of shepherds and travellers, Hermes also escorts men to Hades as Herald of the Gods. Finally the late-comer Hephaestus, a lame smith god, favourite son of Hera, is a mother's son with no father.

Poseidon and Hades

Thus Zeus established his rule as high god. Then the three sons of Cronus divided the inheritance and cast lots for it, Zeus first taking broad heaven and the upper air, Poseidon the sea, and Hades the underworld. But Olympus is common to all, and broad earth. In Thessaly Mount Olympus raises its head into the upper air, and upon it Hephaestus built brazen houses, one for each god. Only Hades never sets foot there: for the gods are immortal and ever young. But in his realm, the sea, Poseidon is supreme and jealous of his brother. He rules it with the fish spear, the trident, with his consort the nymph Amphitrite. In the misty dark lies Hades's house, for the world is a hollow sphere divided by flat earth and girt by Ocean. But in Arcadia icy Styx drips down to Hades. Three terrible rivers join it, wailing Cocytus, painful Acheron and Pyriphlegethon of the burning pyre. There Hades has his realm, king over the dead, hated of gods and men.

Hera and Athena

Zeus wooed Hera when they were still in the house of their parents, winning her by a trick. He turned himself to a cuckoo, and took shelter in her bosom from a shower of rain. Where they lay flowers sprang into bloom, a cloud veiled them, and all earth rejoiced at the sacred marriage of heaven and earth. Hera bore Zeus three children, Ares the war god, Eilythyia who looses women from the pains of childbirth, and Hebe, goddess of youth, whom she gave to Heracles to wife. For the Queen of Heaven loves all brave princes, and protects them in their heroic exploits.

But her husband Zeus she hates, for he has taken other loves, and Athena his virgin daughter he bore unaided. For he loved Metis, 'counsel'. But earth warned him that any son he begot upon Metis would supplant him. So he swallowed her instead, and of his own counsel conceived no son, but a daughter. Hephaestus clove Zeus's head with his hammer, and fully armed sprang Athena with shield and spear, clad in the goatskin aegis with which she protects all warriors, but most of all those of her own city, Athens.

Leto and her children, Apollo and Artemis

Zeus loved Leto, daughter of the Titans Coeus and Phoebe, and she conceived twins. But Hera would not let them come to birth in any land beneath the sun, and sent the Python to chase her from wherever she tried to rest. Poseidon took pity on her, and sent up the holy island of Delos, which floated beneath the waves, and fixed it for ever. There Leto clasped the sacred palm tree and brought forth Artemis, who as midwife at once delivered her brother Apollo. And now no mortal may be born or die on this hallowed isle. Straightway he chased the Python to Delphi, where he slew it with his arrows, and took over the oracular shrine of Earth to tell forth his father's will through his bridge the Pythia. He saved his mother from the giant Tityus. He was born in a cave in Euboea, and at once he grew a thousand feet, and scaled heaven to rape Leto. But Apollo slew him with his arrows: now in Hades he is secured, stretched on his back while two vultures gnaw his liver. Orion was a mighty hunter in Boeotia, he wooed the king's daughter of Chios, but her father blinded him. He strode through the sea to Lemnos, and took a boy on his shoulders, who guided him to the sun's rising. There Dawn gave Orion back his sight, for she loved him for his beauty. But in Delos Artemis slew him with her arrows: the gods are jealous of mortals who aspire to the hand of an immortal. Artemis guards the virginity of her nymphs: no man may look upon them as they bathe after hunting. Zeus loved the fairest of them, Callisto, and took the form of Artemis to seduce her. She bore him Arcas, ancestor of the Arcadians. But Artemis turned her to a bear, and hunted her and slew her with her arrows. As bears, the daughters of the Athenians worship Artemis at Brauron, in saffron dresses. Not even to her brother Apollo would she yield her nymphs. He loved Daphne, and strove for her with a mortal, and put it into his mind to watch her bathing, and Artemis slew him with her arrows. Even so Daphne fled from Apollo, and as he came upon her in his pursuit, she was turned to a laurel. Still he loved her, and made the laurel his sacred tree.

Hephaestus

Hera was angry at the birth of Athena, and to spite Zeus she conceived Hephaestus of herself. But he was born lame, and she exposed him, throwing him out of heaven. He fell into the sea, where Thetis and Eurynome received him, and hid him in a grotto, and taught him smithing, and for nine years he worked there and the stream of Ocean drowned the noise of his smithy. He made fair ornaments for Thetis and Eurynome, out of gratitude to his gentle saviours. Then he made a fair throne, and sent it to Olympus. Hera loved it, and sat upon it, and then found that she could not move from it, with such magic had he fashioned it.

Then the gods sought for the maker of the throne, and begged him to release Hera. But he would not until Dionysus came and gave him wine and made him drunk and brought him back to Olympus on a donkey. Then he was reconciled to his mother, and would save her from the anger of Zeus. So Zeus hurled him at once more from heaven. He fell on Lemnos, where the Sintian men received him, lame smiths like himself. But from there too he came back, and the gods gave him Aphrodite to wife and made him their cupbearer.

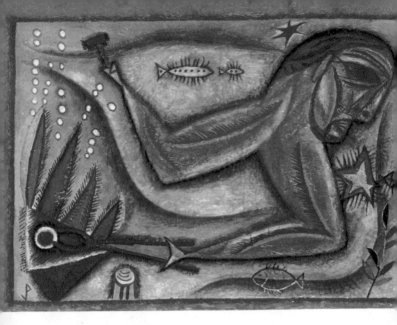

The loves of Aphrodite

But Aphrodite was not born to be a faithful wife. Ares gave her many gifts, and she shamed the bed of her lord. When Hephaestus went to his smithy, she sent word to Ares and he came to her secretly, as he thought. But the Sun sees all, and told Hephaestus and he wrought his revenge. He made a net as light as a spider's web, and hung it from the bed posts, and made off as if for Lemnos. As soon as Ares and Aphrodite were in bed the net came down and held them fast. Hephaestus summoned Zeus and the other gods to witness how he was dishonoured.

Some thought the pleasure worth the price. But Poseidon bade Hephaestus loose the pair, and himself promised to pay the adulterer's fine.

So the gods dissolved the marriage, and Aphrodite loved a mortal, Adonis. He was Myrrha's son, who bore him in incest to her father, and the gods turned her into an incense dropping tree. But Artemis sent a boar to gash Adonis's thigh, jealous that he aspired to the hand of a goddess. Six months he spends with Persephone and six with Aphrodite.

Demeter and Persephone

Persephone was Zeus's daughter by Demeter, and he gave her as bride to his grim brother Hades. But Demeter wanted to keep her daughter and hid the girl in Sicily. Earth created the narcissus, and with it lured her to the valley of Enna, which leads to the underworld. As she picked it Hades carried her off in his chariot.

Sadly Demeter wandered over the earth seeking her daughter: all cities rejected her save Eleusis near Athens, where they cheered her with jests and treated her kindly. Then the Sun that sees all told her where the girl was, and she went to Zeus and demanded her back, in her grief and anger witholding the kindly fruits of the earth. The land became parched and barren, until men and beasts starved and the gods lost their sacrifices.

So Persephone came up again at Eleusis, but each year she goes down again as they store the seed corn. Demeter taught the Eleusinians to tend the corn, tht it may return each year, and to celebrate the mysteries of Mother and Maid. Blessed of men are those who have seen these things.

DEMETER

PERSEPHONE

Hermes

Youngest and craftiest of the immortals is Hermes. Zeus loved Maia and visited her in an Arcadian cave while Hera slept. There in the morning she bore Hermes, and put him in his cradle. But at noon he left it. On the threshold he found a tortoise: from its shell he made the first lyre, and sang to it the tale of his own birth. That night, out he slipped and stole fifty of Apollo's cattle, driving them backwards to sandy Pylos and wearing shoes of plaited twigs to confuse the trail. He made a fire with fire sticks and sacrificed two of the oxen, and hid the rest in a cave. Then home to bed through the keyhole like a mist. When Apollo taxed him with the theft, he denied that a baby could steal cattle, and swore before Zeus that he had never trodden the threshold nor driven the cattle home. Zeus laughed at the crooked oath, and reconciled the brothers, awarding the lyre to Apollo. In it he most delights, leading the muses in dance and singing the tale of his own deception.

Early Man

There is no canonical Greek story of the creation of man. Most myths presuppose that men existed, spontaneously produced by the earth. Many Greek genealogies go back to such an earth-born man, or to the union of a god and the daughter of such a man. Hesiod systematised these generations on a metallic scale of degeneration. He was the first to tell of an age of gold when Cronus was king. Gold men gave way to inferior men of silver, who perished by mutual violence, and were succeeded by men of bronze, the same metal as their spears.

Here genealogy interrupts, and Hesiod interposes the race of Homeric heroes, who fought at Troy and went to the Isles of the Blest. They should really be bronze men, but Hesiod thinks too highly of them. He knows to his cost that he himself lives in the Age of Iron, when shame culture has given way to guilt culture. Outside Hesiod, the gap between genealogy and myth is marked by the flood, which wiped out the earlier and wicked generations of men in much the same way as in the Biblical story of Noah.

But there are also stories in a different style, folk tales intended to explain details of human life. The hero of most of

Above: the gods bring ornaments for Pandora.
Below: actors portraying dancing satyrs. Fifth-century vase painting.

them is Prometheus, son of a Titan and so an adversary of
Zeus. His name was taken to mean 'forethought' and he was
idealized into a culture hero – a clever benefactor of mankind.
He had a foolish brother Epimetheus, an 'afterthought' who
never thinks until it is too late. The ritual of sacrifice, originally
a sacred meal, is explained, like the appearance of heavenly
fire upon earth, by a trick of Prometheus and accounts for the
apparently strange custom of offering to the gods the least
desirable portion of the animal victim. In return, Zeus sends
all the evils of the world upon mankind in the person of
Woman.

The rest of the story of Prometheus and his brother Atlas
belongs to the myth of creation. Atlas is a type of the great
water-walking giant who stands at the ends of the earth at
sunrise or sunset bearing the heaven on his shoulders. A pale
version of this figure, which seems to have played an important
part in some versions of the creation myth, has appeared as the
Boeotian hunter Orion. Prometheus himself has some of his
qualities, and suffers the fate of another such person, Tityus,
the giant who attempted to rape Leto.

Prometheus and Pandora

Men and gods used to eat together. Prometheus killed an ox and divided it into two heaps, and asked Zeus to choose one. He chose the bigger: but it was only bones hidden in fat, and now that is all the gods get for their sacrifices. In anger, Zeus withheld fire from men. Prometheus went up to heaven and stole it, hiding it in the pith of a stalk of giant fennel, as men still carry it smouldering. Zeus was even more angry, and Prometheus warned his brother to accept no gifts from Zeus.

The furious god ordered Hephaestus to make a figure of clay, and Zeus called it Woman: the goddesses gave her all their graces and called her Pandora, 'all gifts'. Epimetheus gladly accepted her: but he was sorry later. Like many men he was bewitched in the presence of beauty and grace, and never considered what might be hidden from his eyes. For Woman is the source of all evil. Zeus had given the brothers a great jar, telling them never to open it. All the world's evils were shut up in it. Pandora opened it and all the evils flew out before she could put back the stopper. Only Hope remained, caught under the lip of the jar – a mixed blessing: for hope often lures men to destruction.

Atlas and Prometheus. Sixth-century Laconian cylix.

25

The Punishment of Prometheus and Atlas

Prometheus and his brother Atlas were Titans. They defended man when Zeus would destroy him, and brought upon themselves the divine wrath. Prometheus held a secret which Zeus was determined to extract from him, and Atlas gave aid to Heracles in his Eleventh Labour.

Prometheus was chained by the angry god to a rock in the Caucasus, where every day an eagle came to gnaw his liver. Every night his liver grew again, for the next day's torture. Zeus knew that the secret would ensure his continued place as master of gods and men. Atlas stood in the western Ocean. He bore two columns which held heaven and earth apart, and guarded the Garden of the Hesperides where the nymphs tended the golden apples of life. Beyond those columns no mortal might pass; Atlas himself went to fetch the apples for Heracles while Heracles shouldered the heavens. Heracles became immortal, and also delivered Prometheus.

For he slew the eagle; and Chiron the Centaur, in anguish from a wound that would not heal, gave Prometheus his own eternal life and died in peace. Athena turned Atlas to stone with the Gorgon's head, but Prometheus she reconciled to

Zeus, and he yielded up his secret. Thus Zeus avoided his father's fate, and ruled for ever.

Phaethon and Lycaon

Zeus still wished to destroy men, and sent a flood. Some say Phaethon gave him the excuse. He was the Sun's child, and persuaded his father to let him drive the chariot. But he could not control it, and set the earth on fire. Zeus put it out with the flood. Others say that Zeus hated the impious bronze men, and that Phaethon fell to his death in the Po: there his mourning sisters, as poplars, drip tears of amber into the river, and from there men bring it to Hellas. Most impious of men was Lycaon, king of Arcadia. Zeus came to his table in the guise of a labouring man, and wanting to make trial of him, Lycaon bade his sons put a baby's flesh in one portion of the sacrifice. But Zeus knew it, and in anger he made Lycaon into a wolf, blasted his sons with the thunderbolt, and overturned the tables. Then he wiped our that impious memory with the flood. But the Arcadians still sacrifice in secret in this manner, and who ever eats the portion of human flesh becomes a werewolf until the next sacrifice.

Deucalion

Thus Zeus overwhelmed the earth with a flood. Yet not all men were drowned in it. For some were led to take refuge in the mountains. The howling of wolves led the people of Lycoreia to a wolf mountain, and the crying of cranes led the Megarians to their crane mountain Geranion. And Prometheus had warned his son Deucalion to avoid the wrath of Zeus. He built a chest, and took into it Pyrrha, his wife, the daughter of Epimetheus and Pandora. In it they floated for nine days and nine nights, and then they came to Mount Parnassus. There Deucalion sacrificed a ram to Zeus Phyxius, the god of escapes, and Zeus sent Hermes the ram god to tell him how to re-people the earth. He bade them cast over their shoulders the 'bones of their mother', but to be sure not to look behind them as they did so. So they cast stones from mother earth with averted eyes, and they became people, men for Deucalion and women for Pyrrha. But Deucalion and Pyrrha had also a natural son, Hellen, father of all the Greeks who are Hellenes, and his son was Aeolus, who ruled in Thessaly.

The cycles of Greek mythology and the heroic genealogies of man

From earliest times the Greeks were concerned to assert their connection with families of the heroic past. Eventually scholars in Alexandria in the third century B.C. fitted all Greek mythology into a systematic framework of genealogies.

In fact all the important myths cluster in cycles around certain places, most of them centres of the Mycenaean civilisation of the second millennium B.C. These cycles formed the subjects of epic poems, of which only the *Iliad* and the *Odyssey* survive. But these heroes know of the great attack upon Thebes in the generation before them, and the mythological history of Thebes was carried back almost to the Flood. To it is attached the saga of Heracles, saviour hero of the Dorians. But Heracles is also an Argive hero, a descendant of the great Argive king Perseus, who slew the Gorgon. Argive mythology is older than Perseus, and it too goes back almost to the flood with Io and her descendants. Thessalian mythology goes back as far, though with fewer generations: it was a descendant of Aeolus

who slew the Chimaera, and another who led the quest for the golden fleece: most of the Argonauts who followed him also hunted the Calydonian boar. The career of Theseus, the great Athenian hero, was in part modelled upon that of Heracles, and Athenian myth touches on that of Crete.

The Greeks practised inheritance from father to son but things are different in the myths. Often the king has no son, or his son is exiled, and he fears to be supplanted by his daughter's husband or son. All steps he takes to avoid this fate fail. His exiled son plays the role of Supplanter in another kingdom, overthrowing the king with his own daughter's help. This recurrent pattern is perhaps to be explained in terms of a society in which kings ruled only for a term in virtue of marriage to the queen.

The children of Io and the tale of Cadmus

The mythology of Argos and Thebes largely ignores the Thessalian story of the Flood. Both places have immigrant founders. Danaus who became ruler of Argos came from Egypt. But he was given a Greek ancestress, Io the priestess of Argive Hera, from whom was also descended Cadmus, the Phoenician founder of Thebes. These stories may possibly reflect foreign influence by way of the Cretans, who were certainly in touch with Egypt before 1400 B.C., and later directly.

But the myth of Io, turned into a cow for love of Zeus, seems to reflect the worship of Hera, who is called 'cow-eyed' in

ZEVS

THRACE

EPIRVS

OLYMPVS ▲

THESSALY

DODONA ■

OSSA

PELION ▲

THESPROTIA

IOLCVS ■

DOLOPIA

PHTHIA

TELEBOANS

PARNASSVS

EVBOEA

DELPHI

ITHACA

CALYDON LOCRIS ■

ORCHOMENVS ■

THEBES ■

MARATHON ■

ACHAIA

ELEVSIS ATHENS ■

CORINTH ■

MEGARA ■

ELIS ARCADIA NEMEA ■

SALAMIS

OLYMPIA ARGOS ■

MYCENAE ■

AEGINA

TEGEA

TIRYNS ■

MESSENE

PYLOS ■

SPARTA ■

SERIPHVS

CYTHERA

CRET

POSEIDON

SALMYDESSVS

BOSPHORVS

HELLESPONT

CYZICVS

MNOS

TROY

PHRYGIA

IDA

LESBOS

MYSIA

ASIA

YROS

LYDIA

ATHENE

CLARVS

COLOPHON

NDROS

CARIA

SAMOS

DELOS

COS

NAXOS

LYCIA

COS

RHODES

SSOS DICTE

Homer. In many stories the gods, especially Zeus and Poseidon, assume animal form to consummate or further their love for a mortal woman. This might be the mythological expression both of the mating of sacred animals and of a sacred marriage in which the King and Queen represented the divine pair. Later Greek knowledge of the Egyptian goddess Isis may have given a new point to the Egyptian connection.

The daughters of Danaus were some of the 'great sinners' exceptionally punished in Hades for killing their husbands. Some other stories about them suggest that they were originally only performing rain magic with their sieves. Greeks often did marry their cousins. The Cretan bull cult was linked to that of Zeus, who loved the priestess Io and changed her into a heifer; he later assumed the form of a bull to carry off Europa, 'broadfaced', a not inappropriate name for a cow. Cadmus too followed a cow when searching for Europa his sister — the same thing described in two mythological ways. But his fight with the serpent, whose teeth he sowed, is a typical exploit to win a divine bride. Cadmus is also said to have introduced writing to Greece, which may have some bearing on his supposed Phoenician origin.

Europe on the bull. Sixth-century vase painting from Caere.

A warrior — Cadmus or Apollo — killing a serpent. Sixth-century Laconian cylix.

Proetus and Acrisius

Now Lynceus was king in Argos after Danaus died, having married Hypermnestra. She bore him Abas, and Abas begot twins, Proetus and Acrisius. These strove in the womb, and when they came of age they fought for the kingdom, arming their followers with shields, being the first to do so. Acrisius the younger won the kingdom by a trick, and Proetus fled to Lycia, and married the king's daughter Sthenoboea. The Lycians restored him to his kingdom, and Argos was split. For Proetus fortified a city at Tiryns, and Acrisius had to be content with the city and plain of Argos. Proetus begot daughters: but when Dionysus came to Argos they would not honour him, and he drove them raving into the mountains. Melampus the Minyan offered to cure them for the hand of one and a third of the kingdom: for he knew the speech of birds and animals. Proetus refused, and all the women went mad and destroyed their children. This time Melampus asked for as much for his brother Bias as well, and gathering a band of men he chased the women to Sicyon and they were cured.

Io

In Argos lived Io, daughter of the river Inachus the son of Ocean. She was priestess of Hera, but Zeus loved her and lay with her, covering the place with a cloud, or himself taking that form. When Hera discovered him, he turned Io into a cow, which Hera begged for her own, and set All-seeing Argus to watch over it: he had two faces and eyes all over his body, so that some were always awake. Zeus sent Hermes, who lulled all his eyes to sleep with his pipe, and then cut off his head, and is called Argus-Slayer, and stole away Io and put her in a herd. Then Hera put Argus's eyes in the peacock's tail and sent a gadfly which found out Io and drove her wandering over all the earth, until she came to Egypt. There Zeus touched her, and she came to her own shape again, and bore a son and called him Epaphus, 'touched'. His children peopled Africa and Asia for his daughter bore twins to Poseidon; Agenor, who went to Phoenicia, and begot Europe and Cadmus; Belus, who stayed in Egypt and begot Aegyptus and Danaus.

The Danaids

Now each of these had fifty children, Aegyptus sons and Danaus daughters, the Danaids. And Aegyptus proposed a match between them, but the daughters of Danaus rejected an incestuous marriage. So Danaus built a ship, being the first to do so, and fled to Argus whence Io had come, and claimed the kingdom. The Argives held an assembly, and Apollo sent a strange wolf to slay an Argive bull, and the assembly accepted the omen, and made Danaus king. The sons of Aegyptus pursued their brides across the sea, and Danaus feigned consent to the marriage.

But he bade his daughters kill their husbands on the wedding night, and bring him their heads. Only Hypermnestra refused, for her husband Lynceus respected her virginity, and she fled with him. But all the others killed their husbands, and they buried them heads apart from bodies to lay their ghosts. And Danaus found them other husbands who would take them without bride price by running foot races for them. But in Hades they are punished for ever, trying in vain to fill a broken pot with water carried in sieves. But Lynceus became king after Danaus.

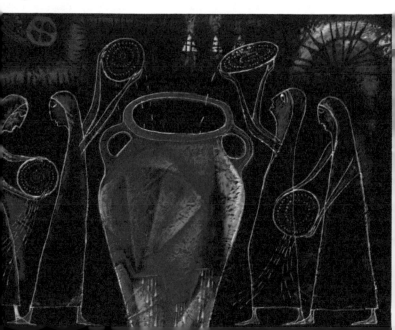

Europa

Agenor, son of Poseidon, went to Phoenicia and begot Europa
and her brothers. Zeus loved her, and came in the form of a
handsome bull where she was playing with her maidens on the
sea shore. They garlanded him, and Europa boldly somer-
saulted over his back, and rode upon him. Then he turned out
to sea and carried her to Crete, and taking the form of a man
begot sons upon her, Minos and Rhadamanthus. She taught
them to leap the bull, as she had leapt upon Zeus, and it is a
sacred rite among the Cretans. Hephaestus made a man of
bronze to guard the island, putting divine ichor into his veins
and sealing it with a nail. His name was Talos and he would
cast himself into a furnace and go round Crete three times each
day: if strangers landed he would sieze them and destroy
them in his fiery embrace. And Rhadamanthus died, and
Zeus took him to the Islands of the Blest, and later he gave
him Alcmena to wife, when Hermes stole her from the bier
at her own death. There he judges the dead with his brother
and Aeacus, the most just of all men, and they assign them due
recompense for their deeds upon earth.

Cadmus

But the brothers of Europa went in search of her at the bidding of their father Agenor. Cadmus went to Thrace with his mother, where she died. Then Cadmus consulted the oracle, and was told to follow the path of a cow, and found a city where she lay down. So in Italy the Samnites vow to the god all those born in a Sacred Year, and when they are full grown, they send them out to found a new tribe, following an ox: and they call the city Bovianum, 'of the ox'. But Cadmus came to Thebes, and there the cow lay down, and he called it Boeotia, 'cow country'. He sent his companions to draw water: but a serpent slew them. So Cadmus killed it, and sowed its teeth in the earth. Up sprang the Sparti, 'Sown Men', fully armed and angry at the death of their dragon father. Cadmus cast a stone among them, and one fought another, and only five survived.

From them descend the best of the Thebans. And Zeus gave Cadmus a wife, Harmonia, daughter of Ares and Aphrodite: for love bears harmony from war. The gods came to the marriage, and they gave Harmonia a golden necklace that Hephaestus made. No good came of that gift to the children of Cadmus.

Dionysus

Dionysus is the only Greek god who is said to have been born of a mortal mother, and who introduced his own cult to Greece after the Flood. This is because, historically, it is a late myth even if it was built upon that of a Mycenaean deity of the same name. Dionysus is made up from two dying vegetation gods, one Thracian and one Phrygian, the latter originally the son of the Great Mother Zemelo. The worship of the Thracian god involved the ritual tearing to pieces of the god himself in the form of a man or an animal, and it gave great emotional release to the worshippers. So did the ritual use of wine in Phrygia, and the re-enactment of the fate of the god in a primitive form of drama. The cult of Dionysus spread rapidly in Dark Age Greece, relieving the tensions of a guilt culture. But a Greek god is all that man would wish to be, immortal and ageless, so he cannot die. So the myths of Dionysus are full of mortal surrogates who suffer on his behalf, fit subjects for tragedy.

Dionysus. i

Semele, daughter of Cadmus, was loved by Zeus in the guise of a mortal and conceived a son, and he promised her whatever she might ask. She was six months with child when, persuaded by the jealous Hera – or prompted by her own folly – she asked Zeus to appear in his true form. His godhead consumed her as by a thunderbolt. But Zeus snatched his son from the fire and sewed him in his thigh where he remained for another three months; thus Dionysus is the Twice-born.

Then Zeus gave the infant to Ino and Athamas who reared him as a girl, to avert jealous fate. But Hera drove them mad; Hermes turned Dionysus into a kid and gave him to the nymphs of Nysa, and in this form he is worshipped. There Dionysus found the vine, and made wine, and gathered a band of followers with whom he travelled over Europe and Asia and even to India. To those who accepted him he gave the blessings of wine but those who rejected him he maddened. Fat old Silenus followed him with satyrs, lustful men with horses' ears and tails, or with goat horns and hooves. Maenads and bacchantes, possessed, handled serpents and brandished the thyrsus, a pine cone on a stick, honouring Dionysus in ecstasy

Dionysus and a satyr.
Detail from a
fifth-century
vase.

Dionysus. ii

First Dionysus came to Thrace, where Lycurgus was the firs
to reject him. For he imprisoned the bacchantes and satyrs
but Dionysus took refuge in the sea with Thetis, mother o
Achilles. Then he magically freed the prisoners, and drov
Lycurgus mad, who, taking his son Dryas for a vine and siez
ing an axe, lopped off arms and legs to prune him. Thus th
land became infertile, and the Thracians took Lycurgus to th
mountains, and tore him apart with horses, and scattered hi
flesh on the fields, so that they bore fruit. Thus they honoure
Dionysus. But he came to Argos, where the daughters c
Proetus would not honour him, and he drove them mad. The
ranged over the mountains, and tore their babes and ate ther
raw. And in Attica he gave a vine to Icarius, who made win
and gave it to the shepherds, wishing all men to share in th
blessings of the god. Fools, they drank it unmixed, like wate
and driven mad they tore apart Icarius. Coming to themselve
again, they recognized the power of the god, and Icarius
daughter, who had been with them, hanged herself from th
sacred tree, honouring Dionysus.

Dionysus. iii. Orpheus

But in Thrace lived also Orpheus, son of the Muse Calliope. He
welcomed Dionysus and joined in his mysteries. Apollo loved
him as a son, and gave him a lyre, with which he made huge
stones rise from the ground and follow him dancing: where
he stopped they are fixed in stone circles. He charmed beasts
too, trees also followed him, and rivers ceased their flow. He
married the wood nymph Eurydice: but Aristaeus loved her
too, and chased her at the wedding, and she trod on a snake
and died before she was made a wife.

Disconsolate, Orpheus followed her to Hades, and he learnt
all that befalls a man after life. With his lyre he charmed
Persephone, and she let Eurydice go, if Orpheus would but not
turn round until he reached the earth. But he looked back and
lost her. Caring for no other woman he wandered with a
Thracian band, preaching the mysteries of Dionysus and what
he had seen in Hades. The angry Thracian women tore him
apart, honouring Dionysus, and cast his head into the river:
and as it floated away down the stream it cried always
'Eurydice! Eurydice!'

Dionysus. iv. Midas

As Dionysus led his band to India they passed through Phrygia, where Midas was king, richest of men upon earth. This was foretold when he was still a child: for as he slept, ants carried grains of corn into his mouth. In his gardens roses grew wild, each of sixty petals and sweetly scented. Here Silenus turned aside and fell asleep. For Midas caught him, mixing wine and water in a well so that he drank deep. Then he feasted him, and learnt all the mysteries of the god, to whom he then returned him, honouring Dionysus and hoping for a boon – which Dionysus granted, whatever he might ask. Midas, ever wishing to increase his wealth, asked that all he touched might become gold. Foolishly, for the gods are bound to grant exactly what they are asked, not more, not less, and even the food Midas put to his lips became gold. Starving, he asked Dionysus to take back the gift. And Dionysus pitied him, bidding him wash in the river Pactolus. Midas did so, and at once the golden touch was washed away. All the sands of the river turned to grains of gold, which the Phrygians gather in fleeces. So the prophecy of the ants was fulfilled.

Dionysus. v

Dionysus returned to Thebes and found his mother's tomb dishonoured. For her sisters said her son was of mortal birth. He maddened them and all the Theban women, driving them to Cithaeron where they routed the troops that Pentheus, grandson of Cadmus, sent against them. But Pentheus cast the leader of the bacchantes into prison – some say it was the god himself. For he was suddenly freed, and he put into Pentheus's evil mind the impious desire to spy on the women. Himself dressed as a woman, Pentheus climbed a tree: but his mother saw him, and tore her son to pieces, honouring the god, and brought his bloody head a trophy to Cadmus. Belatedly they came to their senses, and knew the god. But he took ship to Naxos with pirates, who bound him and would have sold him. Suddenly the mast became a vine, the oars snakes, and the god grew huge among them, and leaping into the sea they became dolphins. At Naxos Dionysus took Ariadne into his triumph, and raised his mother from the dead, calling her Thyone, 'possessed', and came to Olympus and all men honoured the manifest god.

The children of Aeolus

Several mythical motifs appear for the first time in the stories of the children of Aeolus, the Aeolids. The golden ram seems to have been the emblem of sovereignty among a sheep-raising people and in Thessaly the ram was originally identified with Zeus himself.

The ram was sacrificed by the kings, who in times of stress or to stay a threatened disaster would also offer their own sons. They used magic to bring the rain, and among the sheep-raising people was also practised the rejuvenation ceremony, wherein the victim was boiled in a cauldron to make him immortal.

Some of the children of Aeolus suffer for imitating the gods, or for boasting that they were equal to them – they were once divine kings and this impersonation was their duty until in due course they perished at the hands of their successor, probably in the rejuvenation ceremony when the apparently rejuvenated king would in fact be his successor.

Artemis and Actaeon. The Pan painter, c. 460 B.C.

44

Greek thought drew a sharp line between divine and human; it was blasphemy for a man to step over it, and it was properly punished by the gods. Thus what was originally the apotheosis by sacrifice of a divine king, like Salmoneus, or consort, like Actaeon, in the myth is a punishment for presumption.

Other Aeolids seem to be figures in cult. The punishment of Sisyphus suggests a Titan under a mountain; but he is a Corinthian hero and perhaps only artificially an Aeolid. Aeolus is Greek for 'various' and 'son of variety', a possible name for a Master Thief. It is also the name of the king of the winds. The rain magic of Athamas may provide the link here.

Endymion and the Aloads are both types of the handsome hunter like Orion, original consorts of a mother goddess who are later punished for what came to be regarded as presumption. The Aloads are, like Orion, giant sons of Poseidon and try to overthrow the gods like giants in a cosmology. They are also a pair of twins whose paternity is attributed to a god. Normally, only one of such twins is divine, the other the son of the human father. There is a combination of superstition about twins with some device for reconciling descent in the male and female lines. There are similar elements of ritual and sacrifice in the story of Meleager and the Calydonian boar. But it has been completely re-worked to make it the subject of an epic, and is almost unintelligible in its present form.

Ino and Athamas. i

Thus Semele, Cadmus's daughter, was made immortal as the mother of Dionysus. And her sister Ino, wife of Athamas, the gods later made a sea goddess. Athamas, Aeolus's son, ruled at

The Calydonian boar. The François vase, early sixth-century.

Orchomenus, and got for wife Nephele, 'cloud maiden', catching her on the mountain.

But when Cadmus came to Thebes, Athamas took Ino also to wife, and she hated Nephele and her children. So she caused a famine in the land, and Athamas must sacrifice Phrixus, Nephele's son, to Zeus upon the mountain to end the famine and bring rain.

But his mother saved him: she brought the golden ram of sovereignty that Hermes sent to the flocks and on this Phrixus escaped with his sister Helle, flying through the sky. But as they crossed from Europe, Helle fell from the ram, and the strait is called Hellespont, "Helle's Sea'. But Phrixus went east to Ocean where the sun rises. From Ocean flows the great river of Colchis, and there Helios had settled his son Aeetes; his daughter Circe has her home where he sets, in the island of Aeaea in the far west. Aeetes received Phrixus kindly, and gave him his daughter to wife. Phrixus sacrificed the ram to Zeus Phyxius, who puts to flight, and hung the Fleece in a grove. A serpent guarded it.

Ino and Athamas. ii

Thus Ino destroyed the children of Nephele, who returned to the sky whence she came. When Semele bore Dionysus, Zeus gave him to Ino and Athamas, and they reared him in girls' clothes. Even so Hera found him, and Zeus took his son away: for Hera drove Athamas mad, and he took his own son Learchus for a deer, and killed him. They cast him from the land: and if any of the line of Phrixus come to Orchomenus, they lock them up until the feast of Zeus Destroyer, and then they sacrifice a ram and let the stranger go.

The oracle told Athamas to go to a land where the wild animals should entertain him. He came to Epirus, and found a pack of wolves devouring the sheep. The wolves fled at his coming and left him the meat: so he settled there. Ino took her other son Melicertes and boiled him in a cauldron to make him immortal, and leapt into the sea. A dolphin carried the child to the Isthmus of Corinth, where they honour him as Palaemon, 'wrestler'. But Zeus turned Ino into the 'white goddess', Leucothea, for her kindness to the infant Dionysus. With her veil, in the guise of a seamew, she saved Odysseus when his raft was wrecked.

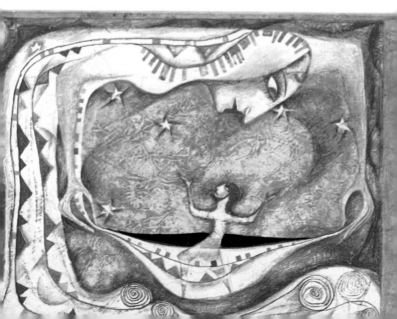

Aristaeus and Actaeon

Cadmus's third daughter Autonoe married Aristaeus. Apollo begot him on the nymph Cyrene, whom he saw wrestling with a lion, and carried off to Libya to lie with him in a golden chamber where is now the city called Cyrene. She taught Aristaeus all useful arts, bee-keeping and olive-growing, and he came to Thebes and married Autonoe. Their son Actaeon grew up to be a mighty hunter. He boasted to be better than Artemis, whom like Orion he wanted to marry. Pursuing her one day with his fifty hounds he found her bathing: so she willed it that she might punish him. Casting water in his face she made him a stag, and set his hounds upon him, and they devoured him. Then they wandered disconsolately until Chiron made them an image of their master; and they guard it. But Aristaeus left Greece, and came to Thrace, and joined Orpheus in his mysteries. But he loved Eurydice, and chasing her at her marriage feast caused her death. And his bees died: for her sister Dryads cursed them. But the gods caused another swarm to spring from the skin of a dead bullock. So he came to Sardinia, and as a rustic deity brings cool winds in the heat of summer, a joy to bees and men.

Salmoneus and Sisyphus

Aeolus's other sons also suffered like Athamas. Salmoneus left Thessaly for Elis, where he founded a city. He hated his brothers Cretheus and Sisyphus, fearing they would have sons by his daughter Tyro to supplant him. But Poseidon lay with her, and Zeus punished Salmoneus for his impious pride. For he claimed to equal Zeus, forcing men to sacrifice to him, and simulating thunder and lightning. For he dragged cauldrons behind his chariot and threw out torches, to bring rain. Zeus heard him, and smote him with a real thunderbolt, and rained out that city. Sisyphus founded Corinth and was the cleverest man in Greece. He outwitted the thief Autolycus, Hermes's son, who changed the colour of the cattle he stole. Sisyphus marked their hooves, and knew his own and got them back. He took Death prisoner, and none died until Ares freed him. Then Sisyphus went with Death: but he made his wife Merope promise to leave his body unburied. Arrived in Hades he complained bitterly about this until Death let him go to punish her, and then come back. He stayed away till he was old! Now he is punished in Hades, rolling a great stone up a hill: and always at the top it falls back again.

Alcyone and Endymion

Aeolus's daughters suffered like Salmoneus. Alcyone and her husband, Ceyx, called each other Zeus and Hera, boasting that their happiness was as that of the gods who punished them for their presumption. The husband they destroyed at sea, with a storm that overwhelmed his ship. Then his ghost appeared to Alcyone, who in mourning cast herself into the sea. Then in pity the gods made them birds, as they themselves appear to men. Alcyone nests on the sea in the winter time, and for seven Halcyon days either side of the shortest day the seas are calm as she sits her eggs.

Calyce bore Endymion, fairest of men upon the earth. The moon saw him hunting on the hills and loved him, and carried him off to Asia. To him the gods gave the greatest happiness: he sleeps for ever in a cave on Mount Latmos, escaping all the ills of mankind. Yet he had been king of Elis, but chose rather to be the moon's lover, and he left the kingdom to his sons to race for in chariots. But a stranger beat them all. But some say that he was admitted to Olympus, and there aspired to Hera's love, and so Zeus cast him into eternal slumber.

The Aloads

Aeolus's daughter Canace bore sons to Poseidon. One of them was Aloeus, 'he of the threshing floor', a king on fruitful Naxos. He married Iphimedia, but she loved Poseidon. Daily she would go to the sea shore and pour sea water into her lap. Thus she bore the god two sons, twins, Otus and Ephialtes, mighty hunters, and they grew apace. It was prophesied that they would never suffer death from other men, or from the gods. Nine years old they were and nine cubits broad, but nine fathoms in height, and they aspired to Olympus, that they might make wives of Hera and Artemis. Ossa they piled on Olympus and Pelion on Ossa, that they might scale the brazen heaven. And they would have accomplished it, had they but come to their full strength. For as it was they caught Ares, and bound him thirteen months in a brazen pot. But their stepmother told Hermes, and he stole Ares away. But Artemis slew them for their presumption before the beard flowered on their cheeks. For as they hunted on Naxos, she sent a hind between them, and each cast his spear, and missed, and hit his brother. So each bore the blood guilt of the other, and the prophecy was fulfilled. So perish all who do such things.

Oeneus and Meleager

Endymion's sons went to Aetolia. Dionysus gave one of them a vine in return for his wife, who bore the god a son. They called her husband Oeneus, 'wine man'; he founded Calydon for his sons and marked the walls with a furrow. One jumped over it, as Remus did at Rome, and Oeneus slew him to keep the walls invulnerable. Oeneus had a daughter too, Deianeira, whom Heracles married, and last of all his wife bore Meleager, it may be to Ares. The Fates told that he should die as soon as the log upon the fire burned through. His mother snatched it from the flames and kept it, hoping to make him immortal. Oeneus sacrificed the first fruits of his vineyard to the gods, but omitted Artemis. Angry, she sent a monster which ravaged the land and the vines. Meleager summoned all the heroes of Greece to come and hunt the Calydonian boar. All came to the exploit, and Atalanta, virgin huntress of Arcadia, who was suckled by a bear. Her father had exposed her because he wanted a son. But Artemis saved her to slay the boar. For nine days the company feasted, and the heroes of Arcadia, Ancaeus and Cephcus, doubted the wisdom of a woman at the chase. But Meleager said that Atalanta must take part.

Meleager and Atlanta

For Meleager, who already had a wife, loved Atalanta, and when he killed the boar, gave her the skin: for she had scored the first hit. But his mother's brothers claimed it by right of kin if he did not want it for himself, and went to war. Meleager killed them in the battle, and his mother cursed him: for her brothers were dearest to her. Meleager locked himself in his chamber with his wife, for fear of death. His father begged him to come forth and save the city, but he would not until it was on the point of capture. Then for his wife's sake he came out, and saved it, and was slain. For his mother put back on the fire the log she had saved from his birth, and when it was burned through, he died. But Atalanta set a foot race for her suitors, and if they lost, she slew them. And Melanion cast golden apples in her path, the gift of Aphrodite, and prevented her pursuit, and so he won her. Yet she called her son Partheno-paeus, 'maiden's son'. But Artemis turned her to a lioness for the loss of her virginity.

The Gorgon. Clay plaque from Syracuse, late seventh-century.

Those who fought with monsters

The conflict of a man or god with a monster has formed the subject of works of art from a very early period. It is sometimes the illustration of a creation myth, or of the annual re-enactment of creation in a New Year ceremony. The Greeks characteristically humanized it, even in pictures of Zeus and Typhon. The myth of the contest between man and monster soon attached itself firmly to two heroes, Perseus and Bellerophon, who take their names, 'destroyer' and 'monster-slayer' from their exploits. The latter is really a Corinthian hero, for Pegasus, his winged horse, comes from there and he is the grandson of Sisyphus. But he was sent to Lycia after refusing the proffered favours of the wife of the King of Argos, and being falsely accused.

All 'virtuous Josephs' consciously refuse the successor's role required of them by an earlier social system. There were Mycenaean settlements in Lycia, where the Chimaera, a monstrous goat usually shown as a lion with a goat's head growing from its back, was to be overcome in a ritual contest for the king's daughter, a disguise for an attempt to get rid of Bellerophon.

Perseus is a similar exile who plays the part of a Supplanter in three different places. First he is the child of the king's daughter, begotten by Zeus in spite of all her father's efforts to prevent it. Mother and child are cast up on the shores of Seriphus in a chest, like the infant Dionysus in some legends. From there he is sent to fetch the Gorgon's head, to get him out of the way, and he does eventually kill the king. But the episode is given a different explanation in the story. Like the Chimaera, the Gorgon has been rationalised. Her mask is an old device to frighten evil spirits, and worn by Athena on her goatskin aegis to terrify enemies. But the Gorgon is only ever represented as a woman, the bride of Poseidon and mother of monsters. She is thus in part a figure in a creation myth. Finally Perseus acquires a bride by rescuing a king's daughter from a sea monster, another variant of the conflict. But he returns to fulfil his fate and kill his grandfather 'accidentally', so avoiding blood-guilt.

Bellerophon and the Chimaera. Sixth-century bronze, probably Etruscan.

Bellerophon. i

Sisyphus's son was Glaucus, whose wife bore two children. But one of these, Bellerophon, was Poseidon's son and one day he slew his brother. He fled to Argos, where Proetus received him with kindness. But his wife Sthenoboea loved Bellerophon, and would have seduced him so that she might then persuade him to kill Proetus and make himself king in Argos. Bellerophon repulsed her, and she went to her husband saying that his guest had dishonoured her: 'Die Proetus! Or kill Bellerophon!' Proetus was ashamed to kill the man who had come to him as a suppliant, and sent him therefore to Lycia, to Sthenoboea's father Iobates. And he gave him a letter for Iobates. Bellerophon found himself received with kindness, made welcome in Lycia and feasted for nine days. On the tenth day Iobates opened the letter, and was appalled to read that he must kill his guest; he could not, no more than Proetus, bring himself to commit such a mean crime. But there was in Lycia a royal beast that ravaged the land, a monster called Chimaera with a lion's head, a goat's body, and a snake's tail. Iobates sought to please his son-in-law and salve his own conscience by sending Bellerophon to fight her, believing he would surely meet his death.

Bellerophon. ii

So Bellerophon prayed to his father Poseidon, who gave him Pegasus, the winged horse born when the Gorgon died. He could not tame him until Athena made a bridle, being the first to do so. Then he mounted Pegasus and came upon the Chimaera and slew her and came back to Iobates having performed that first exploit. Iobates sent him against Solymians and Amazons, enemies of the Lycians. He routed them, performing the second exploit. Then Iobates laid an ambush of the best of the Lycians. Bellerophon slew them all performing the third exploit. Then Iobates knew Bellerophon was a true son of the gods, and gave him his daughter, and he ruled in Lycia. But first he returned to Argos with Pegasus, and carried off Sthenoboea, and cast her into the sea. So he ruled in Lycia, and begot sons and daughters. But in his pride he thought to ride to heaven, and dine with Zeus. But Pegasus cast him off and returned alone to the stables of Zeus. And Bellerophon wandered lame and mad, and ate straw like an ox.

Perseus. i

A daughter, Danae, was born to Acrisius. But he wanted a son
and sought help from an oracle. The oracle told him he would
have no heir, and that he would lose everything to his daughter's
son. So he imprisoned Danae in a brazen house under the
ground, lest any man lie with her; and especially he feared his
twin brother Proetus. But Zeus himself came to her in a shower
of gold that poured into her lap, and she bore Perseus,
'destroyer'. Acrisius shut mother and son in a chest, and cast
it into the sea. But the gods caused the chest to come to
Seriphos, where a fisherman named Dictys took it up in his
nets. He found mother and son alive, and he honoured Danae.
She became a priestess of Athena and Perseus grew up in the
temple. When he was a grown man the king, Polydectes,
visited the temple and desired Danae and would have married
her. He tried to force her to marry him and, wishing to be rid of
Perseus, bade the young men bring him presents. Others
brought him horses, but Perseus was poor and ashamed. Then
Athena inspired him to say that he would get the Gorgon's
head: for she wanted to avenge on Polydectes his insult to her
priestess, Danae.

Perseus. ii

There were three Gorgons, daughters of Phorcys, the old man of the sea, by his sister Ceto, 'sea-monster'. Two of them were immortal monsters: but Medusa the youngest was a beautiful mortal. Poseidon loved her and lay with her twice, once as a horse and once as a man: and he left her his golden sword and swore her to secrecy.

But she told her sisters, and he cursed her and made her like them, with snakes for hair and staring eyes and a great tongue lolling out between huge tusks. If they looked on any one, he was turned to stone. They dwelt in Libya, beyond the streams of Ocean.

It was a hard task for Perseus to find and slay Medusa unharmed. But the gods were with him: Hermes gave him his winged sandals, that he might fly, and Hades the cap of Darkness, that he might not be seen. Hephaestus made a new weapon of adamant, sickle and sword in one, to kill Medusa and cut off her head. Athena gave her brazen shield, to see the Gorgon's reflection only, lest he be turned to stone, and Demeter gave him a magic wallet that never lacked food. Now he was ready for his great task.

Perseus. iii

So Perseus flew away to seek the Gorgon. He came to the land of the virtuous Hyperboreans, who dwell behind the north wind. Ordinary mortals cannot reach them, only god-guided heroes like Perseus and Heracles. They sent him to Africa, and there he found the Graeae, the 'Old Women' who were born grey haired and have but one eye amongst them, which they pass from hand to hand. They were sisters of the Gorgons, and kept watch for them while they slept, lest any surprise them. But Perseus put on the cap of Darkness and as one passed the eye to another he siezed it and cast it into a lake. And each asked 'Do you see anything?' and each answered 'Nothing': for they each thought another had the eye. So Perseus passed by them and caught the Gorgons sleeping, and they did not look upon him. Nor did he look on them: for he held up the shield and looked on the reflection. He slew Medusa with the sword, and cut off her head with the sickle. He put it in the magic wallet and flew away before they woke and saw him: and Athena was with him.

Perseus. iv

But as Medusa died her children were born: first that which Poseidon begot as a stallion, a winged horse. They called him Pegasus, 'springer': for he was born by the springs of Ocean. He sprang up to heaven, and yoked in Zeus's chariot he bears the thunder and the lightning. Athena gave him to Bellerophon, to ride when he slew the Chimaera. Second was born Medusa's mortal son, Chrysaor 'of the golden sword': he took his father's sword and begot three-bodied Geryon, whom Heracles slew in Spain. Athena rejoiced as she heard the dying hiss of the snakes on Medusa's head: inventing the pipes, she imitated the sound. But she saw her distended cheeks in the lake, and cast the pipes away. The satyr Marsyas found them and taught himself to play. He boasted that he could play more sweetly than Apollo could upon his lyre. But Apollo reversed his lyre, and still played, and challenged Marsyas to reverse the pipes and still make music with them. So Apollo was judged the victor and might do to Marsyas what he would. He hung him from a pine tree and flayed off his skin, to teach men not to vie with the gods.

Perseus. v

So Perseus slew the Gorgon and came to Joppa, where he saw a girl chained to a rock by the sea. She was Andromeda, and the queen her mother had boasted she was fairer than Thetis. Poseidon sent a monster to ravage the coast. To gain deliverance the king had to sacrifice his daughter to the beast, and Perseus turned it to stone with the Gorgon's head and won Andromeda for his bride. But her uncle Agenor wanted her, so Perseus turned him to stone as well and then departed for Seriphos with Andromeda. There he found Polydectes about to celebrate his marriage to Danae, and the king jeered at him, asking him what gift was in his wallet. Perseus drew out the Gorgon's head and turned them all to stone. His grandfather Acrisius, recalling the oracle, fled to Thessaly where he married the king's daughter. But then the old king died, and funeral games were held in his honour. Perseus came to compete, and when he hurled the discus the wind took it and it struck Acrisius in the heel and he died of the wound. Perseus returned to Argos to claim his mother's kingdom, but he exchanged it for Tiryns, ruled over by Proetus's son Megapenthes. Perseus founded the city of Mycenae and ruled there.

The heroes of Thessaly

The mythology of Thessaly exhibits a number of very tangled family histories. This may be partly because the surviving versions derive from Greek tragedy. But some things in the story of Cretheus show traces of conflict between the two systems of inheritance, in the male and female lines. Sisyphus is said to have been told that he could be avenged on his brother Salmoneus, who had driven him out, if he had children by Salmoneus' daughter Tyro. In fact, Tyro appears married to Cretheus, the third brother, but bore twins to Poseidon. The twins eventually overthrew Cretheus, whose second wife mistreated their mother. If the kingdom descends in the female line, the king's brother may inherit by marrying his niece. In a patriarchal society, a wife's infidelity, even with a god, is severely punished: a stepmother is a notorious threat to the children of an earlier marriage. Without these two later motifs, Pelias appears as a regular Supplanter, marked by Poseidon as his own son and the true successor.

Admetus is a divine king, upon whose well-being depends the prosperity of his country. He may have been originally

identified with Apollo, in Thessaly also a god of the flocks, but the relationship has been transformed into one of master and servant, and Apollo performs the exploit which wins Admetus his bride. Apollo's service is explained as a penance for avenging upon the divine smiths, the Cyclops, the death of his son Asclepius, a semi-divine figure who exercises the healing powers of Apollo, the plague god. His cult at Epidaurus became very popular in the fourth century.

The story of Bias and Melampus is a folk-tale with sinister overtones: Phylacus may have been sacrificing his son. Centaurs occur in many myths as lustful creatures, half man, half horse, inflamed by wine to carry off human brides. In the sculptures of the Parthenon they are used as types of the triumph of Hellenism over barbarism. Only Chiron is good, and he owes his horse form to Cronus, and not Poseidon. Ixion begot the others on a horse-cloud when he abused the hospitality of Zeus by attempting to seduce Hera. He is a very primitive divine king whose chief duty seems to have been to make fire, rather than rain.

Young centaur. Roman copy of a Hellenistic original.

Alcestis and Admetus. Fourth-century Etruscan vase painting.

Neleus and Pelias

But Tyro daughter of Salmoneus remained in Thessaly where her uncle Cretheus married her: for she gave him title to the kingdom. She bore him sons, Aeson, father of Jason, Amythaon, father of the soothsayer Melampus and his brother Bias, and Pheres, father of Admetus. Then she conceived a passion for the River Enipeus, and Poseidon knew it, and took the form of Enipeus and lay with her, begetting twins, one human, one divine. In shame she exposed them – but Cretheus took another wife Sidero, who treated Tyro harshly.

Poseidon sent a troop of mares to where the children lay, and caused one to mark his true son with her hoof and draw the attention of the herdsman. So that child was called Pelias, 'bruised', and his brother Neleus.

As young men they brought horses to the court of Cretheus, and their mother recognised them by the tokens she had left with them and which they wore. So she set Pelias to slay her persecutor. Sidero fled the temple of Hera and Pelias slew her at the altar and ruled in Thessaly, and doubtless slew Cretheus too, and drove his own brother Neleus to Pylos. But Hera was insulted by the slaying in her temple; she overthrew him by the hand of Jason.

Aesculapius and Admetus

Apollo loved Coronis, grand-daughter of the Muse Erato, and begot Aesculapius. But she took a mortal lover, who would grow old with her. The white crow told Apollo, who cursed it black. But he slew Coronis with his arrows, and snatched his unborn child from the pyre and took him to Chiron. By his mystic birth, Asclepius became a healer, using herbs and the Gorgon's blood. Some he saved from death; others he raised from the dead, robbing Hades of his subjects. Zeus feared lest men became like gods, and smote Asclepius with a thunderbolt; this enraged Apollo who slew the Cyclops who had made the bolt.

In expiation he was bound to a mortal for a year, and he served Admetus, son of Pheres, as a shepherd. Admetus wooed Alcestis, daughter of Pelias: the bride-price was the yoking of a lion and a boar. But the bridal chamber filled with snakes and Apollo drove them out, but he had recognised the sign that Admetus must die. He made the Fates so drunk that they granted that another might die for him. Only Alcestis would: but Heracles wrestled with Death and got her back.

Bias and Melampus

Amythaon married his niece, Phere's daughter, and begat Bias and Melampus. Melampus dwelt in the country, and when his men felled an oak, he saved the young snakes from the nest in it and reared them. They cleaned his ears with their tongues, and he knew the speech of birds and animals. So he helped his brother Bias woo Pero, Neleus's daughter, at Pylos. Neleus required as bride-price the much-prized cattle of Phylacus, son of Aeolus, which were watched over by a wonderful hound which never slept and which nothing could escape. It caught Melampus and he was cast into prison for a year.

One night he heard the worms in the roof saying that next night they would gnaw through the beam. He demanded a new cell, and escaped death. When Phylacus heard the tale he freed Melampus, and asked him to cure the impotence of his son Iphicles. A vulture told Melampus that once when Pylacus was gelding lambs, he stuck the knife in a sacred oak: perhaps he cut mistletoe, and magically gelded his son. The rust of that knife would cure the ill. Melampus got the cattle for his reward, and his brother got Pero for his bride.

Chiron and Ixion

The kindly immortal Chiron had the body of a horse and the trunk of a man. Cronus begot him upon Oceanus's daughter, taking the form of a stallion. He taught all the sons of the heroes, and also Apollo's son Aesculapius, being skilled in knowledge of herbs. He lived among a lustful people, like him in shape but unlike in temper and of different ancestry. Ixion, king of the Lapiths, was their ancestor, a wicked man. He married Deioneus's daughter, promising him many gifts as bride-price. But when Deioneus asked for them, Ixion invited him to a banquet in his house, and dug a pit beneath his chair, and covered it with branches and set it on fire. So Deioneus was burned to death: but Ixion perished in the same way. For Zeus took pity on him at first and purified him of the murder when the other gods refused, and invited him to his table. Ixion repaid him by assaulting Hera, as he thought. But he was deceived, for Zeus had divined his intentions and had made a cloud in Hera's shape, and on it Ixion sired a monstrous creature, Centaur. And Ixion boasted that he had equalled Zeus – who bound him to a fiery wheel which whirled him for ever through the air.

Jason

Now Pelias ruled in Thessaly, robbing Aeson, son of Cretheus, of the throne and making him a prisoner in the palace. But he feared Aeson's son, Jason, whom they sent for safety to Chiron the Centaur, who brought him up under the protection of Hera to overthrow Pelias. Jason was a descendant of Aeolus, and Pelias knew that such a man would bring about his death. When he was come to manhood Jason set out for Iolcus, clad in a leopard skin and wearing one sandal. So they dress in the hills, and the unshod foot grips firm as they fight in the phalanx. When he came to the river, an old woman begged him to carry her over the torrent. Jason bore her across, and when he set her down on the other side she was revealed as Hera, who gave him grace that all women loved him. It may be she made him lose a sandal in the river to fulfil the omen. For Pelias had been warned to beware the single-sandalled man.

When he saw Jason he knew and feared him, but dissembled friendship in his pale heart, and feasted him for nine days and opened his heart to him, asking how best to dispose of an enemy. Hera inspired the glorious answer, 'Send him for the Golden Fleece!'

Centaurs and Lapiths

Centaur lived among the Magnesian mares, whose foals were sired by the wind, so swift were they, and from him arose the nation of Centaurs, whose bestial nature was like their bodies. They seemed men from the trunk, with snub noses and low foreheads: but they lived without laws and preyed upon the Lapiths who lived in the plains. Pirithous was king of the Lapiths, son of Ixion and comrade of Theseus, whom he joined in many impious adventures.

Pirithous took a wife, Hippodameia, and asked the Centaurs to the wedding. They were inflamed by the wine, and one would have carried off Hippodameia, only Pirithous slew him. So arose the war of the Centaurs and Lapiths, in which Theseus joined. Caeneus died in that war, strongest and most impious of the Lapiths.

He was born a woman, Caenis, and loved by Poseidon who then turned her to a man lest any follow him. And Caenis became Caeneus and Poseidon made him invulnerable. Boasting in his strength, he set up his spear and bade the Lapiths worship it. But the Centaurs subdued him, hammering him into the earth with rocks and trees, and so he died.

The voyage of the Argonauts and the Golden Fleece

Jason was sent by Pelias on a quest to the World's End, to recover the Golden Fleece, an emblem of sovereignty. When Jason returned with his bride, Medea, Pelias was boiled in a cauldron to rejuvenate him. The story is a version of the exploit by which the Supplanter is chosen; the emblem of immortality which the hero fetches from the sunrise causes the death of the king: kings are made immortal by sacrificial death. Jason's exploit is also communal and geographical, and both qualities may reflect the situation of the Mycenaean age as well as that of the later period of colonization, when the Greeks penetrated the Black Sea. In antiquity the Fleece was rationalised as that in which the Colchians collected gold dust from a river.

Mycenaean Greece was culturally unified, and communal exploits may reflect the politics of the time. But Jason's crew is also a traditional collection of Helpers each of whom has a special skill to contribute. Many of the adventures they encountered enabled the Helpers display those skills; others explain rituals, and some may be genuine memories of voyages

Jason taming the bulls. Fourth-century Italian vase painting.

of exploration. But much of the saga has been transferred to the *Odyssey* as Odysseys's wanderings between Troy and Phaeacia. There was an annual ceremony of mourning on Lemnos, probably part of a fertility cult that culminated in an orgy like the landing of the Argonauts. A dying vegetation god, Hylas, was annually mourned in Mysia. The Harpies, who resembled both Gorgons and Sirens, may once have been the guardians of the Fleece, and Phineus their sentry, blinded by the Sun because he revealed the way. But they are in the story to enable the sons of Boreas to display their powers, just as Pollux the boxer defeats Amycus. The Clashing Blue Rocks have suggested ice-bergs. But since they destroy the doves which bring ambrosia to Zeus what they protect must be the water of life. The more primitive rituals of son-sacrifice could safely be attributed to Colchians: her brother's limbs, cast out by Medea, are a grim variant of the magic objects cast out in the Flight from the Enchanter. Jason was finally identified with a naval hero at Corinth, where an annual ceremony mourned the death of his children.

The Argonauts. i

So Jason proclaimed his venture for the Golden Fleece, and all the heroes of Greece flocked to win glory. Argus son of Phrixus built a ship, that his father's ghost might be appeased, and Athena set in the bow a talking branch from Zeus's prophetic oak at Dodona, and called the ship Argo and the heroes Argonauts. From Iolcus they sailed by the islands to Lemnos. There they found no men, but women only, whom Aphrodite had afflicted with a foul smell: for they did not honour her. So their husbands took concubines, captive women from Thrace, dishonouring their wives, who killed them every man, husbands, sons, fathers and brothers: all except King Thoas, who was saved by his daughter Hypsipyle. They mourned them until the Argonauts came and landed, and then Aphrodite cured them of their ill, and cast desire upon them, so that they loved them. But the Argonauts left their sons and sailed for the Hellespont. And when the Lemnian women found that Hypsipyle had saved her father, they sold her as a slave to Corinth with her son, where the Seven found her when they came to Thebes. And the Argonauts came to Cyzicus.

Jason steals the Fleece while Medea charms the serpent. Late Roman relief, probably from a sarcophagus.

The Argonauts. ii

At Cyzicus the king of that name, for he had called the city after himself, received them kindly. And the Argonauts put out at night, but meeting with contrary winds made for the shore, not knowing that the land they came to was the land they had left. In ignorance the Cyzicenes joined them in battle, and the Argonauts slew many of them and Cyzicus himself. But in the morning they mourned and buried him. So do the Cyzicenes to this day. Then they put in at Mysia, and the boy Hylas went to a spring for water.

But the nymphs saw him and loved him and drew him down to live with them. When he did not come back, Heracles wandered over the hills seeking him, calling his name. So do the Mysians to this day. Thus Heracles left the Argonauts, and they put into the city of the Bebrycians whose king was Amycus. He compelled all who landed to box with him, and so had put many travellers to death. But after the Argonauts came he never boxed again. For Pollux, one of the twin sons of Zeus and Leda, boxed with him and felled him with a blow.

The Argonauts. iii

Then the Argonauts passed through the Bosphorus and turned north. For they did not know the way to Colchis. They put in at Salmydessus, where the blind king Phineus received them kindly and offered them a feast. But the Harpies came to the table, and snatched away the food and befouled what was left. Then Zetes and Calais rose up, winged sons of Boreas the North Wind, and drew their swords and chased away those foul birds with human heads.

Now it was fated that they should die if they failed of their quarry, and the Harpies too if they failed to escape. So when they came to the Strophades, the isles of turning wind, both were exhausted and they made a pact, and the Harpies swore never to return to Phineus: so both pairs lived. But Phineus in gratitude told the Argonauts the way to Colchis. For he knew it, and had revealed it to Phrixus, and for that he was offered death or blindness, and chose to be blind. But the Sun, father of Aeetes of Colchis, had sent the Harpies against him, for spurning his light and betraying his son. So the Argonauts came to the Clashing Rocks.

The Argonauts. iv

The Clashing Rocks stood at the mouth of the Black Sea, lest any entered and made their way to Colchis, and they let no ship pass through. Not even the doves of Zeus passed them unscathed. When they brought him ambrosia, the food of immortality, from the sunrise, one of them was always lost, and the Father always made up the number. Hera guided the Argo through, first sending a dove, which caused the Rocks to clash together. As they rebounded the heroes rowed in frantic haste and the ship passed through, only losing the tip of the stern. Now the rocks are fixed.

The Argonauts continued eastward, and came to the great river of Phasis and to Colchis. Jason asked king Aeetes for the Fleece and the bones of Phrixus, saying that his ghost could not rest until both were back in Hellas. Aeetes set him exploits; to yoke the brazen bulls, fire-breathing, and sow the dragon's teeth. But his daughter Medea loved Jason, and gave him a magic ointment and told him how to set the armed men who grew from the dragon's teeth against one another by casting a stone amongst them. So she betrayed her father, and with her help Jason performed the exploits.

The Argonauts. v

Then Aeetes plotted to kill Jason. But Medea knew it, and took Jason and brought him to the sacred grove of Ares by night, and with her art she soothed the snake that guarded it, and though he swallowed Jason, yet disgorged him at her bidding. Jason siezed the Fleece, and the unburied bones of Phrixus, and with Medea took them to the Argo and sailed at once down the Phasis. Aeetes pursued them in wrath, for Medea had taken also his son Apsyrtus, and as they gained upon the Argo she slew him and cast his limbs one by one in the path of Aeetes, who had perforce to pick them up for burial, lest his son's ghost haunt him. So they escaped, and sailed to Circe's island. She was the sister of Aeetes, but she purified them after the murder. Up the Danube they sailed and down the Po, and so came to Aeaea. They came too to Africa, and carried Argo over the Syrtis, where Triton met them, and gave a clod of earth to Euphemus, his title to Cyrene.

The Argonauts. vi

So the Argonauts came back to Iolcus with the Fleece, and Pelias received them kindly. But he was Jason's enemy, and

meanwhile had killed his parents – foolishly believing that Jason would perish on his voyage. Medea promised to show his daughters how to make Pelias young again. She boiled an old ram in a cauldron, and used her magic herbs, and a new lamb arose where the old beast had been. The king's daughters Alcestis, Evadne and Amphinome, did the same without the herbs, Pelias died, and Acastus his son buried him and held games in his honour. But he sent Jason and Medea away from Thessaly, and they took the Golden Fleece to Orchomenus and hung it in the temple of Zeus. Then they made their way to Corinth, and there they lived and had children. But the king of Corinth had a daughter, Glauce, who loved Jason, and he gave her to him as wife, that Jason might be his heir. But he got no joy of that marriage, for Medea in anger sent Glauce a poisoned wedding garment, and she put it on, and she was consumed with fire. Then Medea put her children to the sword, and fled to Athens in a chariot drawn by snakes, where Theseus's aged father married her. So Jason ruled childless in Corinth, and dedicated the prow of Argo to Poseidon. He sometimes sat beneath it, remembering, and one day it fell on him and killed him.

The myths of Crete

In the nineteenth century Greek myths were universally regarded as religious fiction. Only the German merchant Schliemann, who taught himself Greek, believed the *Iliad* to be history, and digging at Troy and Mycenae proved that it was, in some sense. Following his example Sir Arthur Evans dug at Cnossus, where Greek mythology placed the Labyrinth. There he discovered a completely new civilisation, called Minoan after the mythological king of Crete. Its relations with the other civilizations of the Aegean are not yet clear, but it appears that in its final stages the great palace at Cnossus was inhabited by a Greek-speaking king. Its complicated plan of passages and rooms have suggested the Labyrinth, the Palace of the Double Axe – the Labrys – which is used as a religious symbol. The which agrees with their developed culture. But the Labyrinth is also a ritual maze through which the king's daughter led her suitor that he might perform his exploit and supplant her father. Athens is as convenient as Mycenae for sailing to Crete, and Athenian mythology is closely linked with Crete. The Athenians claimed credit for the Cretan marvels through the

Athenian Daedalus, archetype of the craftsman for James Joyce. Bulls also feature in Cretan myth from the time of Europa. A number of Minoan works of art show that a form of bull game was really carried out in Crete. Youths and girls apparently attempted hand-stands and athletic leaps on the bull's back, first grasping it by the horns. But one vase suggests that failure was at least as common as success, and death, whether of bull or man, was the desired end of any bull game – in fact or by surrogate the sacrificial death of the sacred king who impersonated the god. Other myths suggest Cretan control of the sea. Some are folk tales full of primitive elements. The dead Glaucus embalmed in honey is made immortal by the herb of life, a ritual description of sacrifice. Nisus's purple hair is his external soul, which makes him invulnerable. But the daughter who betrays him to her suitor is not rewarded by marriage, but punished for treachery as if in a patriarchal society. Minos seems to have been a title of a sacred king who ruled for perhaps a nine-year term, and this accounts for his long reign in myth.

The labyrinth. From a fourth-century coin from Cnossus.

Theseus kills the Minotaur. Detail from the lip of a sixth-century drinking cup.

Minos and Procris

Minos was the son of Europa, whom Zeus, disguised as a bull, carried off to Crete. He quarrelled with his brothers for the kingdom, and Zeus sent a bull from the sea to prove his title. But Minos kept it and did not sacrifice it, and Zeus punished him so that he got no sons. Every woman who lay with him died. It was Procris the wife of Cephalus who cured him. Cephalus was loved by Eos, the Dawn, most amorous of goddesses, and she carried him off; but he pined for Procris. Dawn sent him to test his wife, disguised as a stranger offering gold. Procris was tempted by the gold, to the grief of Cephalus now revealed. In shame she fled to Crete, where she made a woman's shape for Minos. He lay with it and it drew off the poison and he was cured. Minos gave her a dog and a spear, magical things which never missed their quarry. She disguised herself as a boy and took them to Procris. He coveted them, and fell in love with the boy, who was then revealed as Procris. So they were reconciled, for each must forgive the other. The angry Dawn

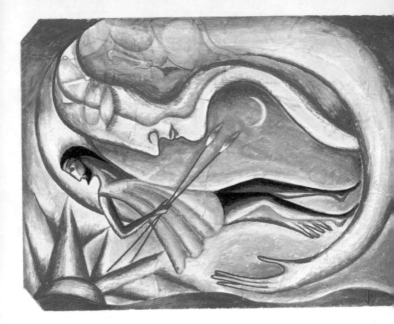

caused the death of Procris. Cephalus went hunting and his wife followed, still jealous, and Dawn caused a noise where Procris was. Cephalus threw the magic spear, and killed his wife.

The sons of Minos

So Minos was cured and had sons and daughters. Yet none survived him. Catreus was killed by his own son, who fled to Rhodes to avoid that terrible fate. But there he slew his sister. For Hermes loved her, and though she fled from him, he caught her by a trick, spreading fresh bull hides before her, and she slipped. Her brother kicked her to death for the dishonour she did him, not believing her lover a god. Catreus came to Rhodes to see his son again, and landed far from the city. The cowherds took him for a pirate, and called his son, who cast his spear and unwittingly killed his father. Glaucus chased a mouse into a jar of honey and was drowned. Minos fetched a prophet, Polyidus, who found his son for him and brought him back to life. He saw a snake bring a herb to revive its dead mate, and the same herb of life made Glaucus immortal. Minos's third son Androgeus was slain by the bull of Marathon.

Talos and Scylla

But Minos built ships and ruled the sea. His land was guarded by a brazen man, Talos: three times a day he cast himself into the furnace and walked the island. If any landed he siezed them in his fiery metal embrace, and burned them to death. But Medea killed him. She soothed him to sleep, and then undid the vein in his leg, and the fiery blood ran out and he died. But Minos sailed against Megara, where Nisus was king. But he could not take it, for Nisus was invulnerable: in his head he had a purple hair among the dark, and in it was his life. None knew which it was but his daughter Scylla. She loved Minos, and made a pact with him, that if she delivered him the city she might follow his ships to Crete. Then she pulled out her father's purple hair and he died, and Minos took the city. But he despised Scylla for her treachery and weakness, and gave her the promised reward for her deeds in a way she could not have expected. Minos tied her by the heels to the stern post of his ship and towed her to Crete and she drowned. Then he captured Athens and exacted tribute; seven maids and seven youths for the Minotaur.

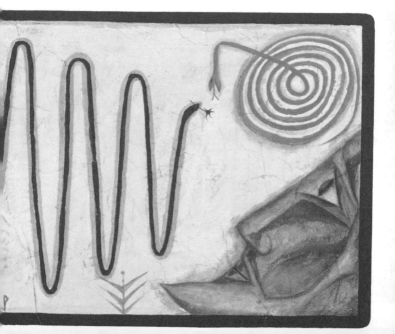

Pasiphae, Daedalus and the Minotaur

For the Minotaur was son of Pasiphae, daughter of the sun and wife to Minos. For she fell in love with the bull from the sea, that Zeus sent and Minos should have sacrificed and which brought such misfortune on his house. But she could not gratify her passion until Daedalus came to Crete from Athens. He was a skilled craftsman, but his apprentice was more skilled, and so Daedalus cast him down from the Acropolis and fled with his son Icarus to Crete, and Minos received him kindly. He built a wooden cow for Pasiphae, and she went into it, and they brought her to the bull. So she had her desires fulfilled, and in time bore the Minotaur, a monstrous man with a bull's head, and he played with men and devoured them. Minos had Daedalus build the Labyrinth, a magic maze of dark passages, and inthe centre of it they shut up the Minotaur. He demanded victims, and drove Minos to war for them, and every year the cities sent youths and maidens, and they shut them up in the Labyrinth, and there they wandered in the dark, until the Minotaur found them and played with them and they died.

The flight of Daedalus and Icarus

But Theseus slew the Minotaur and escaped from the Labyrinth. For Ariadne had given him a clue, which she had from Daedalus. For he remembered Athens, and wanted to return there, and so revealed the secret to help Theseus. But he was not able to return with him to Athens. For Minos knew what he had done, and shut him up in his own Labyrinth, and though he knew the way out he could not escape: for it was carefully guarded.

But by his craft he escaped, though in doing so he lost his son. For he constructed wings, making frames of wood and fixing feathers to them with wax, and with these he taught Icarus to fly, warning him not to approach too near the sun, lest his heat melt the wax, not too near the sea, lest the salt matt the feathers.

But when Icarus rose into the air from the Labyrinth, and saw Cnossus and Crete stretched below him, and the islands, he delighted in the sight, and wanting to see still farther, up and up he flew, heedless of his father's cries of warning. For the sun melted the wax and Icarus fell to the sea on his broken wings.

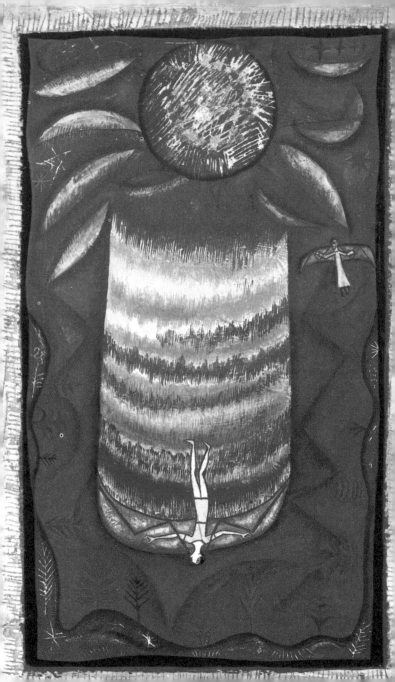

Daedalus in Sicily and the end of Minos

Then Daedalus had no heart to go to Athens without his son. He took ship to Sicily, to the court of Cocalus, who received him kindly. Daedalus built him a treasure house, an impregnable fort stronger than the Labyrinth, at Camicus near Acragas, on the south coast of Sicily. But Minos went through all Greece seeking Daedalus, and came to Sicily and to Cocalus. He carried a spiral shell, and wherever he came he offered great reward for boring a hole in it and threading it. Cocalus gave the shell to Daedalus, wishing to win the reward. Daedalus bored a hole, and stuck the thread to an ant, and so threaded it. Minos knew he had found Daedalus, and demanded that he be given up for punishment. Cocalus agreed, and held a feast, and his daughters took Minos to the bath to make him ready. And there they slew him. For Daedalus led a pipe through the roof, and through it they poured boiling water on Minos, and he died. For seven years the Cretans besieged Camicus, without success, so strong had Daedalus made it.

The myths of Athens and Theseus

Attica had always been poor and isolated from the rest of Greece, and its inhabitants boasted of being born from the earth, like their serpent ancestors Cecrops, Erichthonius and Erechtheus. This isolation may account for the late appearance of the theme of the Supplanter: instead there are recurrent stories of the death of daughters, who fall from the Acropolis to their death or are carried off by the North Wind, perhaps originally from the same place. The legends of Theseus reflect the political development of Athens as the chief maritime power of Greece, interested in dominating the Saronic Gulf by the sea coasts of Megara, Epidaurus and Troizen. The Athenians were also leaders of Ionians against the Dorian Spartans. So the myth of Theseus was modelled on that of Heracles to produce an Attic hero.

Theseus is by name the 'founder' of Athens as the capital of Attica: he persuaded or compelled the local kings to come to Athens and make it the administrative centre. But he started off as the god-begotten son of the daughter of the king of Troizen, and his father Poseidon left his sword beneath a stone as a token of paternity. When the son was strong enough to lift the stone he was of age – ready to supplant his predecessor: it is a kind of exploit. So too Theseus's son Hippolytus, whose death he caused in a tragic story full of overtones of sons supplanting fathers and fathers sacrificing sons, ends up as a Troizenian hero to whom brides dedicated their hair on the eve of marriage. But Theseus had to go to Athens to claim his kingdom, perform his exploit in Crete and win a bride, and return to cause his father's death by inadvertence. His journey from Troizen to Athens by the isthmus road enabled him to perform exploits against decayed giants and establish the Athenian claims. Later he performed further exploits with Pirithous king of the Lapiths, including a descent to Hades from which he had to be rescued by Heracles. He joined in wars against the Centaurs and Amazons who invaded Attica, mythological archetypes of the Athenian defeat of the Persians at Marathon and Salamis.

The old kings of Attica and their daughters

Cecrops the serpent man was born from the earth, and he awarded the land to Athena when she fought Poseidon for it. His three daughters guarded Erectheus, born from the earth when Hephaestus made his assult on Athena. They were

The Parthenon. Athena's temple on the Acropolis seen from the south-west.

Theseus and Amphitrite. The figure between them is Athena. Centre of a drinking cup, c. 500 B.C.

forbidden to open the chest wherein he lay, but two of them disobeyed, and maddened by the sight of a serpent coiled round the child threw themselves down from the Acropolis. One left a daughter, Alcippe, whose father was Ares. Poseidon's son Halirrothius raped her, and Ares slew him.

Erectheus too had daughters, and they all died. Orithyia was carried off by Boreas, the North Wind, as she played by the Ilissus. Erectheus himself made war on the Eleusinians, and they summoned as ally Poseidon's son Eumolpus from Thrace, whose mother was the North Wind's daughter. The oracle promised Erectheus victory if his daughters died; but he would not slay them and they threw themselves from the Acropolis. So their father won the victory, and slew Eumolpus. But this brought down the wrath of Poseidon, who in turn slew Erectheus, whose son Pandion reigned after him.

Tereus and Procne

Pandion had daughters too, Procne and Philomela. He married Procne to Tereus, king of Thrace, to get him for an ally. She bore him a son, Itys. Her sister Philomela came to Thrace to visit her, and Tereus loved her, but she would not yield. He raped her and cut out her tongue, lest she tell her sister.

But she wove cloth in the women's quarters with her sister, and the figures that she wove told her sad story. Then Procne planned revenge on her barbarous husband. She took her son Itys and slew him, and boiled him up in a cauldron, and served him up to his father; and when he had eaten, she showed him the hands and the head. Tereus in madness took up an axe, and chased the sisters from the house, and sought them as far as Daulis on the road to Thebes. There he found them, and might have added two murders to his evil deeds. But the gods pitied them all, and turned Philomela into the nightingale, that ever mourns husband and son, 'Tereu, Tereu, Ity, Ity,' and Procne to the swallow, that cannot speak, and Tereus to the hoopoe, that ever seeks them crying 'Pou, Pou, Pou. Where? Where? Where?'

Theseus. i

Aegeus son of Pandion had no son. When he went to the oracle he was told not to loose the wine skin until he returned home. He went to Troizen to consult Pittheus, who knew the meaning; but Pittheus did not tell it to Aegeus so that his own daughter's son might be the promised heir.

So he made Aegeus drunk, and loosed on him his daughter Aethra, and they lay together. For the child that might be born Aegeus left his sword and sandals beneath a stone as a token. But some say Theseus's father was Poseidon, who came out of the sea. When Theseus came to manhood he raised the stone and took the sword and went to Athens to claim his inheritance. Robbers beset the isthmus road from Troizen to Athens. Theseus slew six of them, labouring to bring the peace of Athens to the land. He spoiled Periphetes of his iron club: he tied Sinis to his own pine trees and tore him apart. He kicked Sciron over the cliff to be prey to his own man-eating turtle, and hammered Procrustes to the bed whereon he used to torture the travellers he waylaid. He was the father of Sinis and men called him Procrustes, the 'stretcher-out'.

Theseus. ii

Thus all these robbers perished by the fates they had inflicted on others. Cercyon, too; Theseus held him in the air until he died. And he slew Phaea, the sow of Crommyon. The people blessed him for bringing order to the land. So he came to Athens. Aegeus did not know him, and did not know that Aethra had borne him a son, and sent him against the Bull of Marathon: but he slew it and returned. Then Medea knew him, who had fled to Aegeus from Corinth and wanted her sons to inherit. She spoke evil words to Aegeus, to persuade him that Theseus meant him harm, and prepared a poisoned cup, with Aegeus's help. But just as Theseus was to drink it, Aegeus recognized his sword, and knocked away the cup, and Medea fled in wrath. But as father and son rejoiced, Minos came to collect tribute for the Minotaur, seven maidens and seven youths. Theseus took the place of one, wishing to free Athens from this slavery. In the ship Minos boasted of his father Zeus, who thundered from a clear sky. Theseus claimed Poseidon, and proved him his father. He recovered a golden ring that Minos cast into the sea. Amphitrite received him in the depths of the sea, and gave it to him and a golden crown.

Theseus. iii

When they came to Crete, Ariadne saw Theseus and loved him, and betrayed her father Minos. She asked Daedalus how a man might get out of the Labyrinth, and he gave her a ball of thread, to save his fellow Athenian. Theseus took the thread, and came to the centre of the Labyrinth, and found the Minotaur and slew him with his bare hands, or with his own sword that Ariadne had given him back.

With the fall of the Minotaur the dominion of Crete over the islands was broken. Theseus sailed with his bride and put in at Naxos. There enchantment came upon him, and he forgot her, and as Ariadne slept he sailed away. Perhaps he feared she would betray him as she had betrayed her father; but however it was, he was soon to face a grief of his own. Dionysus found her on Naxos after Theseus was gone and made her his consort. Then Theseus sailed to Athens with the rescued youths and maidens, and in Delos they danced the Crane Dance to celebrate their escape. But the sails of the ship were black, and Theseus forgot to change them, and as Aegeus watched from the Acropolis he thought his son was dead, and cast himself down and died.

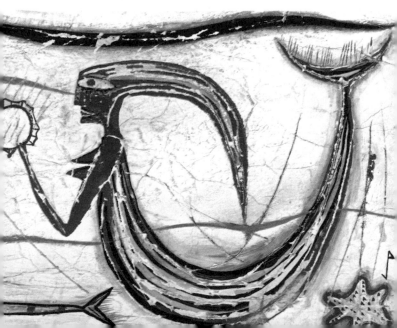

So Theseus, sorrowing, took over the kingdom. But all the heroes accepted him as their peer. He went with Heracles against the Amazons, and brought back Hippolyta as his bride, and called his son Hippolytus. But the Amazons came to recover their queen, invading Attica, and when she would not come they slew her. And Theseus drove them from the land. At the wedding of Pirithous he fought the Centaurs. Then Theseus and Pirithous determined to win the daughters of Zeus; Theseus carried off Helen, and went with Pirithous to Hades to help him win Persephone. She offered them thrones to sit on, and they stuck fast to them. Heracles rescued Theseus when he came for Cerberus. But her brothers took back Helen. Then Theseus married Phaedra, sister of Ariadne. She saw Hippolytus, and loved him, but he would not, for he was vowed to Artemis and hunted with her. Phaedra accused him to Theseus, and hanged herself for shame. Theseus called down the wrath of Poseidon on his son, and as Hippolytus drove from Troizen Poseidon sent a bull from the sea and wrecked the chariot, and Hippolytus died. Then Theseus went to Scyros, and there he fell to his death.

Theban mythology

A second myth of the foundation of Thebes did not involve Cadmus. The twins Amphion and Zethus were old cult figures at Thebes, where their tomb was the goal in a ritual conflict between Thebes and Phocis, where lay the tomb of their mother Antiope. Each year the Phocians tried to steal earth from the Theban tomb to sprinkle on their own, to make the land fertile. Since Dirce, their mother's tormentor, was torn to pieces by a bull and cast into a sacred spring, the twins may have been connected with the worship of Dionysus in that form. But they have been given a complicated tragic story made up of elements from other myths. The later myths of Thebes are also best known in tragic form. Sophocles used the history of Oedipus and his sons to express his deepest thoughts about guilt, responsibility, identity and the laws of god and man. Freud has added psychological depth to the myth, and made it perhaps the most significant of all for modern man.

Amphion and Zethus bind Dirce to the bull. Roman copy of a Hellenistic original.

Its mythical origins are simple. Oedipus is the Supplanter who performs an exploit to win a bride and a kingdom. Only because, to suit patriarchal customs, the kingdom he wins is his father's, do the elements of parricide and incest emerge. They were quite foreign to the earlier system of inheritance, and in most other myths have been softened by making the Supplanter the grandson of the king, and that in the female line.

The story of the attack on Thebes by the Seven, and their successful sons ten years later, has been joined on to this story by introducing the enmity of Oedipus's sons. It seems to be a genuine saga of an Argive attempt to check the power of Thebes with Calydonian help. In the course of the two expeditions Amphiaraus of Argos and Tydeus of Calydon meet ritual fates: the former became an immortal hero, but Greek taste rejected the method by which the other originally achieved it. Alcmaeon's matricide, also the subject of a lost tragedy, reflects the conflicting duties of two forms of society. In all the myths Tiresias is prominent: he retained intelligence in Hades, the mark of a buried and not a cremated hero.

Amphion and Zethus

When Pentheus died, Cadmus and Harmonia went away to the land of the Illyrians and were turned into serpents. And Lycus and Nycteus ruled: for they were of the Sown men. Nycteus had two daughters: one bore Labdacus to the son of Cadmus, and the other, Antiope, was loved by Zeus. Great with child she fled to Sicyon, and Nycteus feared the unborn child, and killed himself. His brother Lycus avenged him. He sacked Sicyon and brought back Antiope, and kept her in chains, and Dirce his wife tormented her. But Antiope bore twins, Amphion and Zethus, and exposed them on Cithaeron, and a cowherd found them. Zethus he reared as a cattle breeder, and Hermes gave a lyre to Amphion. One day Antiope's bonds broke of their own accord, and she came to her sons, and made herself known to them. And they slew Lycus. But Dirce they tied to a bull which dragged her to death, and they cast her dead body into the spring which bears her name. Then they fortified Thebes, which was not walled before then. The stones came to Amphion's lyre and formed themselves into a wall.

Portrait of a dead warrior. Detail from a fifth-century Athenian grave vase.

Oedipus. i

But Laius son of Labdacus they cast out. He went to Elis, the land of Pelops, and carried off Pelops's son Chrysippus, being the first to practise such love. So he was warned by the oracle to have no son of his own when he succeeded to the kingdom of Thebes. But he forgot the oracle when he was flushed with wine; he begot a son whom the royal couple, fearing, exposed with his feet pierced. But the baby was taken to the childless king of Corinth, who called him Oedipus, 'Swell-foot', and brought him up as his own son. Oedipus went to Delphi, and learned that he would kill his father. He swore to avoid Corinth, and where three roads meet he met a man in a chariot, who thrust him from the path. Oedipus slew him, ignorant who he was, and came to Thebes, and learned the king was dead. The Sphinx had come to the city, and strangled all who failed to solved her riddle. Oedipus told her what goes on four feet at morning, two at noon and three at eve: for it is man. So the Sphinx hanged herself. But Oedipus they hailed as saviour, and he married Queen Jocasta, Laius's widow, and became king of Thebes.

Oedipus. ii

Thus Oedipus married his mother, and ploughed the field where he was sown. But the gods brought all to light, sending a plague on Thebes until Laius's killer was revealed. Oedipus led the hunt for himself, bringing down curses on his own head, and when he knew his fate, he blinded himself. Impotent, he dwelt in Thebes until his sons Eteocles and Polynices came of age and shared the kingdom. But Eteocles drove out his brother, and Oedipus cursed them both, and Antigone led him to Athens where the gods claimed their own. Polynices went to Argos, where he met Tydeus, son of Oeneus, and they fought. Adrastus of Argos saw the emblems on their shields and recognized the omen. So he gave his daughters to Theban lion and Calydonian boar, promising to restore both to their kingdoms. Seven heroes he mustered, one for every gate of Thebes. The seer Amphiaraus refused: for he knew that all who went would die except Adrastus. So they bribed his wife Eriphyla with the necklace of Harmonia, and reluctantly he went at her bidding. But he bade his sons avenge his death upon her.

Seven against Thebes

Thus the Seven against Thebes were doomed from the start.
They came to Nemea at the isthmus: and Hypsipyle from
Lemnos showed them a spring. But as she left the king's son, a
serpent slew him, first of the deaths in that war. So they called
him Archemorus, 'Beginner of Fate', and for him they founded
the Nemean games, where the judges wear black and only
soldiers' sons may compete for the mourning crown of parsley.
Then they attacked Thebes, and the bold Capaneus boasted he
would take it though Zeus forbade it: and for his impious boast
he was smitten by a thunderbolt. Then all fled save the two
brothers, and they killed each other and fulfilled their father's
curse.

Athena would have made Tydeus immortal for his bravery:
but she saw him with his enemy's head, eating the brains, and
Athena let him die in disgust. Zeus with a thunderbolt cleft the
ground as Amphiaraus fled, and swallowed up his chariot, and
his mighty ghost gives oracles. Adrastus alone escaped on his
divine horse Arion, which Poseidon got as a stallion on
Demeter, when she hid among the mares. And he came to
Athens and Theseus received him.

The Epigoni and Tiresias

Jocasta's brother Creon now ruled in Thebes, and he honoured
Eteocles's body: but Polynices he bade them leave a prey for
dogs and birds. But Antigone buried him, honouring the laws
of the gods: for a brother is closest of all men to his sister. And
Creon impiously walled her up to die unwed. Too late he
repented and broke open the tomb: for Antigone had hanged
herself, and Creon's son Haemon, killed himself for love of her.
Thus the line of Labdacus died out.

Ten years later the sons of the Seven came back to Thebes,
led by Alcmaeon, son of Amphiaraus. This time Thebes yielded
to them: for Tiresias knew it was the will of Zeus. He was a
nymph's son, and following his mother he came upon Athena
bathing, who struck him blind. But for his mother's sake she
opened his inner eye, giving him the gift of prophecy in
exchange for impotence. He knew all human things. For he
struck two snakes coupling, and was made woman. But Hera
made him man again: for he told Zeus a woman enjoys more of
the pleasures of love: so she punished him. The last deed of
Tiresias was to tell the Thebans to yield, and they obeyed him
before he died.

Alcmaeon

After Thebes was taken, Alcmaeon returned home to take vengence on his mother for his father Amphiaraus's death. He took the necklace of Harmonia with which they bribed her, and killed her. She cursed him with her dying breath. The Furies pursued him, for they reckon descent only by the mother, caring nothing for the father or his fate. So Alcmaeon went mad, and fled to Psophis, and married the king's daughter Arsinoe, giving her the necklace.

But the earth would bear no fruit for the presence of the matricide, and they drove him out. Nor might he escape the Furies in any land that had existed when he did the deed. So he settled on the islands freshly laid down at the mouth of the river Achelous, and married the river's daughter Callirhoe, 'Fair Stream'. But she wanted the necklace: so Alcmaeon asked Arsinoe for it, pretending he must dedicate it to Apollo. Her brothers learnt the truth and murdered him and took back the necklace. But Callirhoe prayed that her infant sons might avenge their father's murder. They at once grew to men, and slew the murderers, and themselves took the necklace to Delphi. Thus it came back to the gods.

Amphitryon. i

The sons of Perseus reigned in Mycenae and the cities of Argos.
But they quarrelled. For Hippothoe, the daughter of Mestor,
son of Perseus, was carried off by Poseidon and bore him
Pterelaus, who called his people Teleboans, 'Far Cry'. Pterelaus
was invulnerable: his soul was in a golden lock of hair, and
his sons claimed Mycenae as Mestor's portion. But Mestor's
brother Electryon ruled it. So he went to war with the Teleboans, leaving his land, his cattle and his daughter to his wife's
brother, Amphitryon, son of Alcaeus, son of Perseus, making
him swear to keep Alcmena virgin. But when he came back
Amphitryon slew him, by accident or in a quarrel: perhaps he
had broken his vow and meant to keep the kingdom.

Amphitryon went into exile in Thebes, where Oedipus was
dead and Creon was regent. And he delivered Thebes from a
monstrous vixen sent by Dionysus, to which they exposed
their sons as to the Sphinx, and which could never be caught.
But Amphitryon set on it the marvellous hound Laelaps, that
Procris had of Minos, when she cured him, and it never failed
of its quarry. So the gods turned hound and vixen to stone,
thus resolving an impossible contest.

Amphitryon. ii

Then Creon consented to join the war against the Teleboans,
for Alcmena would not consummate her marriage with Amphitryon until he avenged her brothers, killed by them. And
Cephalus came too. And Comaetho, daughter of Pterelaus, fell
in love with Amphitryon, and for his sake she pulled out her
father's golden lock, and he died. Amphitryon promised to
keep Comaetho as long as she lived, and he kept his promise:
for he lay with her and then killed her for her treachery, and
returned to Thebes and gave the land to Cephalus. But when
he came, Alcmena at first rebuffed him, saying he had returned
already. For Zeus had come in his shape, wishing to beget
another mighty hero of the line of Perseus and making the
night three times as long for the forging of Heracles. But then
she bore to Amphitryon Iphicles, the mortal twin of Heracles.
When the time came, Zeus swore that the Perseid born that day
should rule Mycenae. But Hera cheated him, holding up the
birth of Heracles by magic knots until Eurystheus was born to
the wife of Sthenelus son of Perseus. Thus Heracles served
Eurystheus all his life.

Heracles

Heracles has been grafted on to the mythology of Thebes by making the Perseid Amphitryon leave Mycenae through a complicated history in which he plays the Supplanter in several different places. There seems to have been a Theban hero Alcaeus, 'Strong', identified with Heracles by interpreting it as a patronymic and giving Heracles a grandfather Alcaeus. Alcmene was also a Theban heroine and the object of a cult. But Heracles's only Theban exploit was slaying the lion of Cithaeron, the skin of which identifies him, and fathering fifty sons in a night, as a folk hero of enormous appetites should. His return to Mycenae was explained as exile for killing his children (presumably once a sacrifice), and the Labours as penitential service to Eurystheus. Tiryns, by the sea, may once have been subject to Mycenae in the hills. Heracles's name, 'Glory of Hera', is contradicted by her hostility. For he has become Zeus's bastard, hatred by the lawful wife, and his servitude is put down to her schemes. He was probably once the son of the mother goddess who helped him in his labours –

Heracles fighting Geryon. From a vase painting by Euphronios.

as Athena does Heracles. Many of these Labours are located in
the Peloponnese; the lion at Nemea, the Hydra on the Argive
gulf, the birds and boar in Arcadia, the hind in Achaea and
the cowshed in Elis. They are all monsters, and like the exploits
of Theseus may reflect political claims – or even drainage works
of unknown antiquity. Others are farther afield in Crete or
Thrace, and the rest are superhuman quests – that for the gold-
en apples of immortality, for instance, and the harrowing of
Hades. Most heroes only perform one or at most two of such
exploits. But Heracles was the patron of the invading Dorians,
who claimed descent from his sons, and so he has taken over
what were probably once the tasks of local heroes, and has
been enlarged into a general Deliverer of Mankind. Many of
his deeds are almost supernatural, and at times, as when bearing the pillars of Heaven, he seems a figure in a creation myth.
Indeed, the battle of Gods and Giants was postponed in order
that Heracles, who has a position in the heroic genealogies,
might be the human Helper, and he was eventually received
into Olympus in myth if not in cult.

Heracles. i

Hera hated Heracles, though he bore her name and though she suckled him. For Zeus lulled her to sleep and Hermes put the babe to her breast. But he bit her and awoke her, and she thrust him off, spilling her milk across the firmament as stars. Then she sent snakes to the cradle of the twins. Iphicles fled, but Heracles strangled them. And he grew in strength and appetites. At eighteen he slew the lion of Cithaeron, whose skin he always wore, and begot fifty sons in one night on the fifty daughters of Thespius. But when his mother Alcmena died Hermes stole her from the bier, and put in a stone which the Thebans reverence, and took her to the Islands of the Blest. Creon gave Heracles his daughter Megara as prize for valour in battle. But Hera pursued him with madness and he slew his children, and was sent to Tiryns to serve Eurystheus for penance, who set him labours, first ten and then two more. First he slew the Nemean Lion and brought its skin to Tiryns. But Eurystheus feared him, and hid himself in a brazen jar under the earth.

Heracles carrying off the tripod from Delphi. Fifth-century Greek vase.

Heracles. ii

Second he slew the Lernaean Hydra, a swamp monster born to Typhon and Echidna, with nine heads, and where one died, two grew: 'Even Heracles cannot fight two!' Hera sent a monstrous crab from the swamp to bite his heel. So he called Iolaus to sear the roots as each of the Hydra's heads was cut off. Third he caught the Golden Hind of Artemis, that had gold horns, pursuing it to the land of the virtuous Hyperboreans, who dwell behind the North Wind and sacrifice asses to Apollo when he visits their circular stone temple. There he got the olive he planted on Olympia. Fourth he caught the great Erymanthian boar alive, lodging with the Centaurs who gave him wine but then fought him in drunken madness.

He drove them off, accidentally wounding the good Chiron, who prayed to die, immortal though he was, for the pain of the Hydra's poison on the arrow. Prometheus exchanged mortality with him, and Chiron died, and Zeus put him in the stars. Fifth he cleared the cowsheds of Augeas – for they were not stables – for a tithe of the cattle. Heracles did it easily, foul though they were, diverting two rivers through them, Peneus and Alpheus.

Sixth he drove away the man-eating birds from the Stymphal-
ian Lake, scaring them with brazen castanets which Hephaestus
made for Athena. Seventh he brought the Cretan bull, which
Poseidon sent and which begot the Minotaur, and he set it free
and it went to Marathon. Eighth he brought the man-eating
mares of the wild king of Thrace, Diomede the son of Ares,
which tore men apart in honour of Dionysus. Ninth he was
sent for the Girdle of Hippolyta, Queen of the Amazons, who
dwell in Asia Minor.

These were warlike women who lived alone without men,
only meeting their neighbours once a year to conceive children,
of whom they reared only the girls, cutting off their right
breasts lest they hinder them in war when they drew the bow
and hurled the javelin.

Ares gave Hippolyta her girdle for her prowess in war. But
she fell in love with Heracles and would have loosed it for him
in love. Only Hera stirred up the Amazons to fight him, and
fearing treachery he slew Hippolyta, and loosed her girdle in
death and took it. And on his way back he came by Troy, and
found it terrorised by a sea monster.

Heracles. iv

For Laomedon had hired Poseidon and Apollo to build invulnerable walls for Troy. But mortal Aeacus helped them, and there the walls were breached when Troy was beseiged. So Laomedon refused their reward, and they sent the monster, to which Laomedon exposed his daughter Hesione. Heracles saved her: but Laomedon cheated him too of his reward, and would not give him the famous horses Zeus gave in return for Ganymede, whom he carried off to heaven to be his cup-bearer: for he was a pretty boy. So Heracles vowed to come again to Troy for revenge.

But then for his tenth Labour he went to Spain to fetch the cattle of Geryon. At Gibraltar he set up the Pillars of Heracles, where he divided the land: in Ocean beyond men may not sail. But Heracles threatened the sun, who gave him his golden bowl to sail in. Ocean sent waves to swamp it: Heracles frightened him too and came to Geryon and slew all three bodies of the giant, and took his cattle. Then Eurystheus gave him two more Labours: for he would not count the Hydra and the Cowsheds.

Heracles. v

These last two Labours were the greatest. First he went west to Libya, for the Golden Apples of the Hesperides, which grew where Zeus first lay with Hera: nymphs tended them, and a dragon guarded them. On the way he met the giant Antaeus, whose strength was renewed each time he touched the earth: so Heracles held him in the air until he died. Atlas got the apples for him, while Heracles held up the globe of heaven: for no mortal might visit the garden. When Atlas came back, he would not take up his burden again. But Heracles asked a moment's relief while he got a pad fo his shoulders; he siezed his chance, picked up the apples and fled. Atlas was turned to stone by Athena with the Gorgon's Head, when she returned the apples to the garden. Last of all Heracles harrowed Hell, and went down to Hades to fetch Cerberus, the three-headed dog that guards its gates. There he found Theseus and Pirithous, and rescued Theseus. But he left Pirithous, who had impiously attempted to win Persephone. Thus Heracles paid his debt to Eurystheus, and took Cerberus back to Hades, and returned to Thebes.

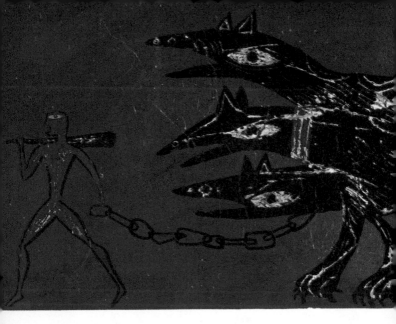

Heracles. vi

There he gave Megara to Iolaus, and himself wooed Iole, daughter of Eurytus, a great archer who offered her as prize to the man who beat him, as Heracles did. But Eurytus would not give him Iole, he remembered now the grief of Megara, and feared lest he kill his children again. In mad anger Heracles slew Eurytus's son, Iphitus, and went to Delphi to be purified, and when the Pythia would not answer him, he stole the Tripod, and fought Apollo for it until Zeus intervened and parted them, and made it clear that Heracles would pay for both crimes.

So Hermes sold him into bondage to Omphale, Queen of Lydia, and he served her for three years, dressed as a woman to deceive the ghosts: but he got a son on her. Then he fulfilled his vow to sack Troy, taking Telamon who breached the wall where his father Aeacus had built it. Heracles was jealous, so Telamon made an altar to Heracles Victor. The mollified hero gave him Laomedon's daughter, allowing her to take with her any captive she chose: she chose her brother, ransoming him with her veil and calling him Priam, 'Bought', whom Heracles made King of Troy. But Hera sent storms and blew Heracles to Cos, from where Zeus saved him.

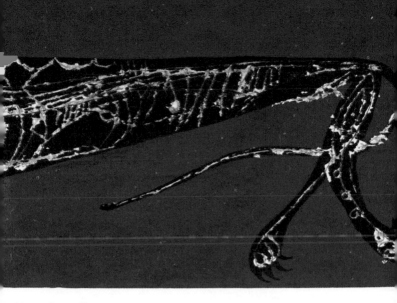

Heracles. vii

Athena brought him to the Phlegraean Plains in Thrace, where the gods were fighting with the giants. For Earth still grudged Zeus his victory over the Titans, and, impregnated by the blood of Uranus, in due time bore giants, huge and invincible: for they could perish only at the hands of a mortal.

In Thrace there grew a herb which would make them immortal, but Zeus forbade Sun and Moon to shine lest Earth find the herb, and picked it himself and hid it away, lest men too become like gods.

Zeus brought his son Heracles into the fight as his mortal ally, and he slew the giants with his arrows – Alcyoneus, who stole the cattle of the sun, and Porphyrion, who would have forced Hera. So the gods defeated the giants.

And Heracles engaged in many wars: he captured Elis, and there founded the Olympic Games, planting the sacred olive he brought from the Hyperboreans. At Pylos he slew all the Neleids but Nestor. He wounded Hades in that fight, and struck Hera with an arrow on the breast that he had bitten as a baby, and he gashed Ares himself in the thigh. Thus that mighty hero fought with the gods.

Heracles. viii

Heracles came to Calydon to marry Deianeira, Meleager's sister. The river Achelous loved her, and wrestled with Heracles for her in the form of a bull, until his horn was broken. At the marriage feast Heracles accidentally slew the cupbearer; he found it hard to measure his strength. Sadly he acknowledged his crime and retired into exile. He came with Deianeira to a river where the centaur Nessus carried Deianeira over on his back. On the far bank he tried to rape her, and Heracles killed him with an arrow. Nessus told Deianeira that if Heracles but put on a shirt anointed with blood from the wound, he would never love another woman. When Heracles went to Oechalia and sacked the city and captured Iole, whom Eurytus had refused him, and sent her back to Trachis, Deianeira feared that she had lost his love. She sent him the shirt of Nessus, and when Heracles put it on, it clung to his skin and burnt his flesh. And learning what it was he knew his fate: for he was to die at the hand of no man living. And he built a pyre on Mount Oeta and was carried up to heaven and reconciled to Hera, who gave him Hebe, goddess of youth, for wife.

The children of Pelops and Aeacus

The house of Pelops, like that of Oedipus, provided material for tragedy. The poets saw the fate of Agamemnon, Clytemnestra and Orestes as the working out of a family curse brought upon the house by Pelops if not by Tantalus. The latter is one of the divine kings, like Athamas, who dine at Zeus's table, and serves up to the gods his own son boiled in a cauldron.

The golden fleece also appears in the myths of the Pelopids, associated with Hermes who gave the sceptre to Pelops, first of the shepherd kings of the Peloponnese. As always in Greek myth, an obsolete or repugnant ritual is re-interpreted in terms of divine retribution. Similarly, Pelops came to Elis as a Supplanter to win the king's daughter in a ritual contest which was 'arranged' with divine approval to bring about the death of the king. Myrtilus the charioteer, Hermes's son, seems to be a surrogate, given access to the queen and then killed in place of the king. It is his death, rather than that of Oenomaus, which triggers off the curse.

The story of Phoenix is an expurgated story of a similar surrogate who escaped after castration. Twin kings occur in

other myths. Thyestes may have been the son of Hermes as Myritilus. Dual kingship may also be a device for reconciling patriarchal inheritance with a kingdom held in the female line. For each generation the kingdom is exchanged, as the son of one king marries the daughter of the other, and in the end grandson sits on grandfather's throne.

In the story of Atreus and Thyestes the motifs of sacrifice and exposure are recombined. A ritual by which the dead king was torn in pieces and sprinkled on the earth, may perhaps be inferred as the means by which Atreus proposed to keep the letter of his oath.

Aeacus, like Admetus, is the just king whose welfare is the kingdom's. The mountain where he prayed catches the storm clouds over Aegina; his men dug marl from pits and then lived in them. Peleus is a virtuous Joseph rewarded for his chastity: Thetis a figure from the succession myth; if Zeus had married her he would have been overthrown by their son. As it is, she has become the mermaid-bride in a folk-tale.

Tantalus

Tantalus, king of Lydia, son of Zeus, was blest by the gods with wealth and prosperity above all men. They admitted him to their feasts and councils. Yet he abused the trust they placed in him. For he stole nectar and ambrosia from their table and gave it to men, wishing to make them immortal and sharing with them divine secrets. He committed perjury also. When Pandareus stole the golden dog from Crete, that had guarded the infant Zeus, he took it to Tantalus, who, when asked for it back, swore before Zeus that he had never had it. Finally he asked the gods to a feast, and, wanting to make trial of them, served up his own son Pelops boiled in a cauldron. All the gods knew and refused the impious food, save Demeter, grieving for Persephone, who chewed a shoulder. Then at last the gods punished Tantalus, casting him down to Hades where he stands thirsty in a pool of water. But as he bends to drink it drains away, and when he reaches up for the grapes over this head, they are snatched from his grasp. Always over his head hangs Mount Sipylus, ever threatening to fall upon him.

Pelops carries off Hippodameia. Fifth- century Greek vase.

Niobe

Tantalus's daughter was Niobe. She married Amphion the lyre player, who with his brother Zethus overthrew Lycus and fortified Thebes. She bore him seven sons and seven daughters, and rejoicing in her glorious fecundity she boasted foolishly that she was more fortunate than Leto: for Leto had but twins. Niobe did not reflect what manner of twins those were. For they were gods, Apollo and Artemis, who, jealous always for the honour of their mother, came against the children of Niobe with their arrows and slew them all but one: and they lay unburied for nine days. The gods buried them on the tenth day. The single child they spared was Chloris, whom they honoured for her piety: Neleus married her and took her to Pylos where she was glorious in her children. For Apollo granted to Nestor all the years of which he and Artemis had deprived his mother's kin. He saw three generations of men fall as the leaves, and went to Troy. Amphion in impious anger attacked Apollo's temple, and Apollo slew him. But Niobe, all tears, went back to Lydia, and prayed to Zeus, who turned her into a stone upon Mount Sipylus, and there she still weeps for her children, and warns mortals to know their place.

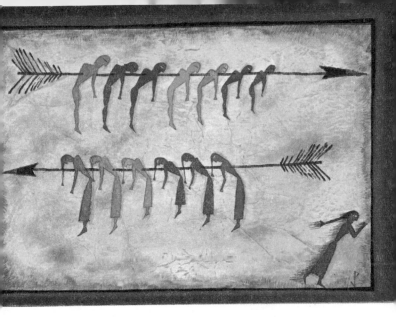

Pelops

The gods gave Pelops an ivory shoulder for the one that Demeter gnawed. He wooed Hippodameia, daughter of Oenomaus, king of Elis, who was Ares's son, and like Evenus set her suitors a chariot race, driving his father's horses in full armour. and nailing the losers' heads to his house, while he barbarously threw their bodies down anywhere, unburied. For he feared that his daughter's son would supplant him, and wanted to marry her himself.

But Poseidon gave Pelops a winged chariot: for he loved him. And Hippodameia bribed Myrtilus, Hermes's son, to replace the pins that held her father's chariot wheels with wax ones. On the turn they sheared through, and Oenomaus was torn to pieces by his own horses, and dying cursed Myrtilus, and Pelops killed him. So Pelops ruled in Elis. And he made war on Stymphalus, king of Arcadia. When he could not defeat him, he feigned friendship with him, but at the feast he treacherously slew him, tearing him to pieces and scattering his flesh upon the fields, honouring the god. But Greece was cursed with drought for Pelops's treachery, until Aeacus prayed to Zeus, who sent rain. For Aeacus was must just of men.

Atreus and Thyestes. i

So Pelops ruled all Greece below the Isthmus, and called it Peloponnese, 'Pelops's Island'. For Hermes gave him the sceptre: yet in the end he took vengeance on the house of Pelops for the death of Myrtilus. Hippodameia bore two sons, Atreus and Thyestes. But Pelops loved more his own son Chrysippus, whom he had begotten on a nymph.

Hippodameia, fearing for her own children's right to the throne, urged her sons to kill Chrysippus, and they cast him into a well. Pelops cursed them and drove them out. But when he was dead they ruled Elis. Now the kingdom was his to whose flocks Hermes sent the golden lamb of sovereignty. It came to Atreus, who killed it and hid the fleece. But Aerope his wife loved Thyestes, and stole the fleece and gave it to him, and he cast out Atreus, saying he might be king again when the sun went backwards and set in the east. For Tantalus's sake, Zeus brought that portent to pass, and Atreus ruled again. Pretending to be reconciled to Thyestes he made a feast and set meat before him, and Thyestes ate. Then Atreus showed him the heads of his children, whose boiled flesh he had eaten, and cast him out. Thyestes laid a curse on the house of Atreus.

Atreus and Thyestes. ii

Thyestes knew he would be revenged if he begot a son on his own daughter, Pelopia. Hiding his face, he surprised her: but she secured his sword. Atreus married her, and when she bore Thyestes's son, she exposed him. Hermes sent a goat to suckle the child, and Atreus saved it, thinking it his own. They called him Aegisthus, 'Goat Boy'.

Famine came to Elis for Atreus's crime, and would not end until Thyestes returned to the kingdom. Atreus feigned friendship, but cast him into prison and sent Aegisthus to kill him. He meant to cast his body in pieces on the fields, thus returning him to the kingdom and honouring the god. Thyestes recognised his sword in Aegisthus's hand, and Pelopia, knowing who was her son's father, stabbed herself with it. When Atreus saw the bloody sword he rejoiced that Thyestes was dead. But Aegisthus slew him for the victim at the sacrifice, and restored his father. Agamemnon and Menelaus, Atreus's sons fled to Aetolia where Tyndareus of Sparta had married the king's daughter. When Heracles restored Tyndareus they came with him, and he gave Agamemnon Mycenae. Menelaus got Helen, and he ruled Sparta after Tyndareus's death.

Aeacus and Peleus

Aeacus was the most just man in Hellas, as his grandson Achilles was the mightiest of those who went to Troy. He was the son of Zeus by the nymph Aegina, to whom Zeus gave the island that bears her name. When Aeacus prayed for company, Zeus turned the ants into warriors, called Myrmidons. He had sons Peleus and Telamon, who at the discus killed their bastard brother Phocus, the seal-maiden's son. Telamon went to Salamis and begot Ajax: Peleus to Phthia to Eurytion, whom he killed accidentally at the Calydonian Boar-hunt, and went to Iolcus with Acastus.

At the funeral games for Pelias, Acastus's wife saw Peleus as he wrestled with Atalanta, and loved him and would have lain with him. But he would not, and for his chastity the gods chose him as husband for Thetis. Both Zeus and Poseidon wanted her: but Prometheus revealed that her son would be mightier than his father, so lest the gods be overthrown they gave her to a mortal. To win her consent, Peleus wrestled with her, holding her firm in all her disguises. She could not escape him though she hurt him badly, and finally she yielded. But she would never speak to him.

Childhood of Achilles

The gods came to the wedding of Peleus and Thetis. But Eris, 'Strife' cast among them a golden apple inscribed 'For the fairest'. This became the cause of the Trojan war. But Thetis bore children to Peleus, and she made them immortal in fire. So with her last born, Achilles, but Peleus interrupted her, and she broke her vow of silence and had to leave him and go back to the sea. Achilles had been made all invulnerable except for his heel, which was burnt away and not yet replaced. Peleus gave him a mortal bone, and there Achilles was wounded to the death. Some say that she dipped him in the Styx, holding him by the heel.

So Peleus dwelt alone, and gave Achilles first to the centaur Chiron to rear, and then to Phoenix. Chiron made him strong and courageous, but Thetis loved her son, and knowing that he was fated either to die young and glorious at Troy, or live at home unrenowned, sent him to Scyros and hid him among the the women dressed as a girl. There he begot Neoptolemus on the King of Scyros' daughter. But Odysseus came as a pedlar, and blew a trumpet, and Achilles threw off his woman's clothes and leapt to arms.

Phoenix

Phoenix, who cared for Achilles after Chiron, dandled the boy on his knee at feasts, and cut for him the choicest morsels of meat. For he had no son of his own. He was Amyntor's son in Old Hellas. His father took a concubine, and Phoenix lay with her, and his father cursed him, and made him impotent, that he have no son of his own. He would have fled: but his kinsmen constrained him. Nine days they feasted him, and at night they barred his chamber door, and kept watches by the fires outside his door and in the fenced courtyard. But on the tenth night Phoenix broke the doors, and found his guards overcome with sleep in the arms of the women. For he had given them unmixed wine. So he leapt over the fence and escaped, and was not made a victim of his father's anger. He came to Phthia to the court of Peleus, who received kindly the man who could beget no son to supplant his host, and made him lord over the Dolopians, and sent him to Troy to protect Achilles and teach him to be a speaker of words and a doer of deeds.

The children of Tyndareus

The children of Tyndareus are exceptional in Greek myth for the manner of their conception and birth. Tyndareus himself is a figure in the heroic genealogies, a Perseid on his mother's side and an Aeolid on his father's. The four brothers are linked to Calydonian mythology, an unexplored region evidently important in Mycenaean times. Idas and Lynceus are a pair of Helpers who joined the Argonauts. Idas also features in two rituals: in one he wins a bride in a chariot race in which the loser and his horses are thrown into a river. In the other he strives with Apollo for his bride: perhaps he originally impersonated the god, but the story has been moralized.

From Calydon, Tyndareus brought Leda back to Sparta. Since her daughter Helen is unquestionably a decayed Spartan Tree-goddess, and her sons Castor and Pollux, the great Dioscuri, or Youths of Zeus, rather gods than demi-gods, it may be conjectured that Leda too was once a goddess, possibly cognate with Leto, and a mother-goddess whom Zeus visited as a swan, the bird form favoured by Mycenaean deities. Since

Leda and the swan. Late Roman sculpture.

she laid two eggs she was presumably a swan too, a bird later sacred to Apollo. The Dioscuri seem to be faded gods rather than deified heroes, if the distinction is valid. Their cult was Dorian, and extremely popular in Sicily and south Italy, from where it reached Rome, or at least Lavinium, at a very early date, attested by an early inscription.

In Sparta the cult was symbolized by a wooden yoke of twin beams, perhaps originally a sacred tree, like their sister Helen. They ride upon white horses, carry off the daughters of Leucippus, 'White Horse', and support Dorians and Romans in cavalry battles, at Lake Regillus and the Sagra. Later they were identified with the constellation Gemini, and as St. Elmo's Fire saved sailors at sea. But they may have started as fertility gods whom the fruitful earth held alive.

In myth they are twins, only one of whom is divine, the other being a mere mortal's son. In their encounter with Idas and Lynceus, a folk tale in which those two make use of their special talents, one is slain, and it is a mark of the fraternal affection of Pollux that he insists on sharing his immortality with his mortal brother.

Idas and Marpessa

Noble were the sons of Gorgophone, Perseus's daughter, whom he named 'Gorgon-slaughter' for his great exploit. Aeolus's son Perieres married her, and ruled in Messene, and begot four sons, Aphareus and Leucippus, Tyndareus and Icarius. Aphareus married Arene, and on her he begot Idas and Lynceus, marvellous brothers. Lynceus had the keenest sight of any man: Idas had the greatest appetite, and could eat faster than fire consumes. He wooed Marpessa, daughter of Ares's son Evenus, who set her suitors a chariot race and nailed the losers' heads to his house.

Idas did not fear the skulls he saw: Poseidon had given him a winged chariot, so he won and carried her off. Evenus chased him to a river. Idas's chariot flew over it: but Evenus's could not, and he slew his horses in a rage and cast them in the river, and himself too, and it is called by his name. And Idas flew over the sea and came to Messene. There Apollo would have stolen Marpessa: for he loved her. But Idas fought him. Zeus parted them, letting Marpessa choose her husband. She chose Idas, fearing lest Apollo desert her when she grew old.

Leda

But Tyndareus was driven from Sparta by Hippocoon, and fled to Aetolia. There he married Leda, daughter of Thestius, brother of that Evenus whose daughter Idas won. But Hippocoon fought against Heracles at Pylos, who in revenge led the Tegeans against Sparta. And they feared their city might be taken in their absence: but Heracles gave the king's daughter a lock of the Gorgon's hair, which Athena gave him, for she loved the Tegeans.

This lock of hair, held up three times from the walls would save the city: for the enemy would flee, or all be turned to stone. So Heracles sacked Sparta and restored Tyndareus and Leda. But Zeus loved Leda for she was of the stock of Ares, and came to her as a swan, as he had gone to Hera as a cuckoo, and in that shape he begot twins. The same night also Tyndareus lay with Leda, and she bore two eggs, in each a mortal and an immortal twin. From one came Helen, like to the immortal gods in beauty, and her sister Clytemnestra, whom Agamemnon wed. And from the other came Castor and Pollux, the great Dioscuri, that is 'The Youths of Zeus'.

Castor and Pollux

Pollux the boxer was immortal and Castor the spearman mortal: but they loved each other as brothers should. Theseus carried off Helen for her beauty and because she was daughter of Zeus. For her and Pirithous the Lapith made a compact to help each other to such marriages. When Theseus went with Pirithous to Hades to carry off Persephone Castor and Pollux rescued their sister. Then, wanting to marry, they carried off the daughters of Leucippus 'White Horse' from their wedding feast. The bridegrooms Idas and Lynceus kept their grudge, and went cattle raiding with their cousins Castor and Pollux, and cheated them of the spoil. For half was to be his who ate his portion first, and the rest to the second: and Idas ate both like fire. Then Castor and Pollux lay in wait for them. Lynceus with his keen sight spied Castor, and Idas slew him, and stunned Pollux when he killed Lynceus. So Zeus struck Idas dead. But Pollux shared his immortality with his brother. Alternate days in heaven and earth, riding on white horses, the Heavenly Twins bring help to warriors and to mariners.

The binding of Talos. Fourth-century vase painting.

Odysseus and the wooing of Helen

All the kings of Greece came to woo Helen, wanting to be son-in-law to Zeus. Tyndareus feared to favour one over another, until Odysseus counselled him what to do. He exacted an oath from all the suitors to help the chosen groom if he were wronged, and gave Helen to Menelaus, son of Atreus, and the kingdom of Sparta with her. Then he made his brother Icarius yield his daughter Penelope to Odysseus, who had won her in a foot race. But Odysseus would not stay in Sparta, and went back to Ithaca, and Penelope chose to follow him rather than stay with her father, being the first to do so.

She bore Odysseus a son, Telemachus, and when they came for Odysseus to join the Trojan War, he pretended to be mad, and yoked an ox and an ass to the plough, and sowed his fields with salt. But they laid Telemachus in the furrow, and when the ox would have trampled him, Odysseus turned the team, and was seen to be sane.

So he came to Troy, and it was he who found Achilles when he was hid among the women, and was the craftiest of the Greeks who went to Ilium.

The tale of Troy

The tale of Troy is the only piece of Greek mythology part of which has survived at length in an epic. The language used by Homer, made up of fixed poetical formulae, provided a vehicle for the oral transmission of fact over long periods of time. From Schliemann on, men have hoped to prove that Homer is history. Certainly Troy was a fortified palace site from the beginning of the Bronze Age. It had links with Greece from 1900 B.C. and was sacked in about 1250 B.C., a period when the Hittite empire in Asia Minor was crumbling and a number of revolts are attested in their archives. But although Troy was the subject of some traditional poetry, the *Iliad* has joined to it other traditions that had originally nothing to do with it.

The *Iliad* is a straightforward and humanized account of the fighting at Troy: it does not mention the sack though it implies it, and personifies the two forces in the two great heroes, Hector and Achilles, whose duel may have been once a ritual pursuit, since Achilles is traditionally 'swift-footed'. All the episodes in the siege have been fitted into a plot that only occupies a

The wooden horse. Detail from a Corinthian vase, early sixth-century.

Right: Achilles kills Penthesilea. Fifth-century vase painting.

few days, a feat of literary organization performed in Ionian
Asia Minor perhaps about 800 B.C. There the migrants recalled
their heroic past, and found in the siege of Troy a theme that
dignified the struggles they had had to establish themselves.
The Greeks were never as conscious of Hellenic identity as
when fighting barbarians, Persians at Marathon and Salamis,
and conquering them under Alexander the Great. Thus, though
there was a city Troy, and it was sacked, it was not Homer's
Troy, and the *Iliad* is not the story of that sack. Consequently,
the mythology of events before and after the siege is only alluded
to in the poem. It was later collected in minor epics which
filled in the gaps, and provided themes for tragedy.

The Trojans were always very close to the gods, to whom
sons are sacrificed and daughters married, and who build its
walls, invulnerable except where a mortal helped. Aeneas
certainly and Paris possibly are sons of a goddess who makes
the latter irresistible to women. There are also many folk-tale
motifs in the conditions to be fulfilled before Troy can be taken.

Paris and the Trojans

For Helen's sake was fought the Trojan War. The goddesses
strove for the golden apple which Eris had cast at the wedding
of Peleus and Thetis, and asked Paris, son of Priam, to choose
the fairest. He was a shepherd on Mount Ida. For they exposed
him when they learnt that he would be the bane of Troy: and
his mother dreamed that she had brought forth a fire-brand.
There Paris defended the flocks, and was called Alexander,
'Defender', and there he married Oenone. But Aphrodite
promised him Helen; he gave her the apple, rejecting Hera
who promised him power and Athena who offered wisdom.
For Aphrodite loved the Trojans for Aeneas's sake, whom she
bore to Anchises. And Dawn carried off Priam's brother
Tithonus, and begged immortality for him. The grudging gods
gave only what she asked, and Tithonus withered away into a
grasshopper with old age; all his senses faded with his
vigour, and yet he cannot die. And Apollo loved Cassandra,
Priam's daughter, and gave her prophecy for her favours. The
gods cannot recall their gifts: but angry when she refused him,
he swore that she should never be believed. So close are the
Trojans to the gods: but even Zeus could not save Troy.

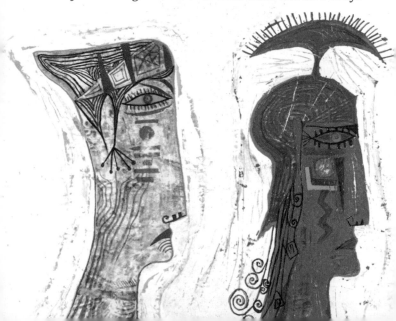

Philoctetes: Telephus. i

So with Aphrodite's help Paris carried off Helen, and Menelaus
reminded the suitors of their oath, and they mustered under
Agamemnon, king of Mycenae, his brother. Swiftly they sailed
for Troy: but the gods delayed its fate. First they came to
Lemnos, where they left Philoctetes, who had the bow of
Heracles: for his father lit the pyre for Heracles when all others
refused. Apollo sent a snake, which bit Philoctetes, and the
wound would not heal, and for its foul smell the Greeks left
him behind. For Apollo knew that without the bow of Heracles
Troy could not be taken.

Then the gods sent the Greeks to Mysia, where Telephus was
king, and the Greeks believed that they were at Troy. Heracles
begot Telephus on Auge, to whom he gave the Gorgon's lock
at Tegea. Her father sold her into Mysia, exposing the child
for fear he would die at his hand as an oracle warned. Telephus
was saved, and fulfilled the oracle, and fled speechless to Mysia
and found his mother. Then he routed the Greeks, but was
wounded by Achilles, tripping in a vine. For he had not
honoured Dionysus, and the wound would not heal, and the
whole land was sick with its king.

Telephus. ii: Sacrifice of Iphigenia

The Greeks mustered again at Aulis in Boeotia. Telephus came there as a beggar in rags: for the oracle told him that only the wounder could heal his wound. He promised to lead the Greeks to Troy, and Achilles touched his thigh with the spear, and he was healed and the land was barren no more. The gods sent omens to the Greeks: a snake ate the nestlings in the sacred plane tree, and two eagles tore a pregnant hare. Calchas the prophet knew that the Greeks would consume ten years in the war, and that Artemis required a sacrifice for Troy: for winds from Thrace held back the fleet. Agamemnon was the leader and they looked to him to provide a worthy gift for the goddess. They overcame his natural reluctance, and in his name they sent for his daughter Iphigenia, saying that she should marry Achilles, and Clytemnestra let her go. But they sacrificed her to Artemis, who snatched her away, putting a deer in her place, taking her to Crimean Tauris to be her priestess and sacrifice all shipwrecked Greeks. The winds ceased and the Greeks came to Troy. Menelaus won a single combat with Paris for Helen: but Aphrodite saved him and the Trojans refused to give up Helen, and the war began.

The Iliad. i

Helen came to the walls of Troy, and grieved to see the Greeks. But for her beauty the Trojans bore her no grudge. She named the Greek leaders for Priam, Agamemnon and Menelaus, Telamon's son Ajax, Tydeus's son Diomede, crafty Odysseus and Nestor, wisest of the Greeks, who had seen three generations of men fall as the leaves. But her brothers she did not see: for they were dead.

Nine years the Greeks besieged Troy, sacking the cities around it. Achilles slew the father and brothers of Andromache, wife of Hector, Priam's son, and he became all of these to her. Achilles slew the boy Troilus, who was fated to save Troy if he grew to manhood. The Greeks sacked Chryse, and took the priest's daughter and gave her to Agamemnon. But Apollo sent a plague on the army, and Calchas bade him give back the girl. Agamemnon in wrath took Briseis, whom Achilles had won as his prize, and Achilles thought to slay him, only Athena restrained him. He swore to fight no more. So Thetis begged Zeus to give victory to the Trojans, that they might have need of her son, and his glory be the greater.

The Iliad. ii

But Agamemnon mustered his troops for battle. Menelaus and Paris fought for the hand of Helen – but Aphrodite saved the wounded Paris out of the battle in a mist. Then Athena prompted the Trojan archer Pandarus to break the truce, and he shot at Menelaus. Then she inspired Diomedes, and he fought Ares and wounded Aphrodite, sending her crying to her mother Dione: but with Glaucus he exchanged armour, for they were ancestral friends. Then Hector bade his mother pray to Athena for Troy, bringing a robe to her image: but the goddess was implacable. Hector bade farewell to his wife and child, and went to the battle, and fought Ajax, and led the Trojans against the wall around the Greek camp. Agamemnon repented of his quarrel, and sent gifts to Achilles, but he spurned them. Then Hector breached the wall and would have fired the ships, had not Poseidon rallied the Greeks in despite of Zeus. But Hera tricked her husband, getting love charms from Aphrodite. She went to Zeus on Ida and he loved her, and slept. But when he awoke in anger he sent Poseidon back to the sea, and Apollo to help the Trojans, and they fired the ships.

The Iliad. iii

Then Achilles smote his thigh, and bade Patroclus arm himself and save the Greeks. So he put on Achilles's armour, all save the ashy spear of Peleus, that only Achilles could wield, and he thrust back the Trojans in rout, and slew Sarpedon, son of Zeus, who caused the heavens to weep for him, and then Patroclus would have taken Troy before its time, only Apollo slew him and gave the glory to Hector. They fought over his body, and Hector spoiled it of its arms and put them on. Then Achilles in his wrath came back to the battle. Hephaestus gave him newly-made armour and Athena made him terrible, and he fought the river Xanthus, and finally met Hector in single combat. He chased Hector thrice round the walls of Troy and slew him, and dragged his body behind his chariot. But the gods preserved it from harm, and sent Priam under escort of Hermes to ransom it. Priam paid a huge sum, and kissed the hands that had slain his son, and Achilles pitied him, for he was like his own father who would mourn for him. So Priam took the body and thus they buried Hector, the tamer of horses.

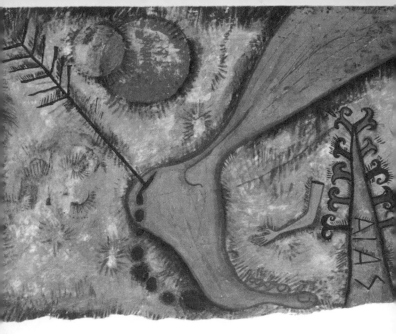

How Troy would fall

And the Trojans brought allies, Africans from the East, and
Memnon son of Dawn led them, a swarthy hero. But Achilles
slew him, and he lies by the Hellespont. Yearly, birds mourn
him and sweep his tomb. The Amazons came too, and Penthesilea their queen, who had killed Hippolyta at Athens.
Achilles slew her, but he honoured her body, though Thersites
said otherwise, and put out her eyes with his spear. For that
Achilles slew him though he was Diomedes's kin, and there
was dissension in the Greek camp. But the gods exacted Hector's
death of Achilles: Paris shot him in the heel, where alone he
was vulnerable: Apollo guided the shaft. They gave his arms
to Odysseus, rejecting Ajax, though he was the best of the
heroes after Achilles. Ajax killed himself, and they buried him
by Troy, and when Odysseus was wrecked the arms of Achilles
were swept to the tomb. The hyacinth grows there, a flower
inscribed with the hero's name, AIAS. Thus died the two great
Greek heroes, and the Greeks despaired of their enterprise and
would have sailed away from Troy and cheated fate. But the
Trojan Helenus revealed how Troy would fall.

The taking of Troy

For Paris died by the bow of Heracles, without which Troy could not be taken. Philoctetes had it, marooned on Lemnos; but at Calchas's bidding they fetched him, and he killed Paris. Then Helenus would have married Helen, but they gave her to Deiphobus his brother. He went to Ida, and there Odysseus captured him, and he told how Troy should fall. First the Greeks returned to Asia the bones of Pelops, son of Tantalus, taking them from his tomb at Olympia, where the chariots race in his honour. Then Odysseus took Diomedes, and disguised himself as a beggar, and they stole the image of Athena, the Palladium. Helen knew him, but she yearned for Greece, and so she helped him. Then they brought Neoptolemus, Achilles's son, from Scyros where he begot him when he hid among the from Scyros where he begot him when he hid among the women, and he led the heroes in the wooden horse, which they left on the shore, an offering to Athena, and sailed away. Laocoon warned the Trojans, but Apollo sent snakes to devour him and his sons, and the Trojans dragged in the horse. That night it dropped armed men, and Troy was taken.

After the fall

There lies over the siege of Troy, as over the other communal exploits of the Greeks, an air of misfortune. This may reflect the actual situation at the end of the Mycenaean period, when the eastern Mediterranean was in a turmoil of wandering tribes and freebooting expeditions. These even reached Egypt, where names in a victory inscription may be those of the Achaeans and Danaans. The Mycenaeans had freely settled in this area, and this over-extension weakened their hold on Greece.

So most of the heroes returned to find trouble at home, usurpers in their kingdoms. Only Nestor and Menelaus returned safely, the latter after a long period of trading in Egypt, where a later account said that Helen had spent the war, thus saving her divine credit: they fought for an image at Troy. Some stories accounted for ceremonies; for a thousand years Locrian maidens made their way to Troy to serve in the temple if they entered undetected – otherwise to be put to death. An old ceremony thus justified links between Locris and Troy, and was explained as penance for Cassandra's rape by Locrian Ajax. The prophetic battle between Calchas and Mopsus is propaganda for the Ionian oracle of Apollo at Clarus.

The two great return stories are those of Odysseus and Agamemnon. The *Odyssey* already knows Orestes's murder of Clytemnestra as a meritorious deed, to be imitated if necessary by Telemachus. Both young men were asserting the patriarchal system of inheritance against the view that marriage to the widowed or deserted queen gave title to the kingdom. The *Odyssey* was conceived as a sequel to the *Iliad*, and goes to pains to tell the fate of most of the heroes. But it includes motifs from the Argonautic saga, and there are many elements from the myth of the Supplanter. (Nausicaa is the princess to be won by the stranger prince, and only the plot stops Odysseus marrying her. He becomes the consort of the witch Circe after protection by a herb that must once have been the Herb of Life.) The story of Electra and the fate of Orestes has been worked over by the tragedians, concerned with guilt and responsibility and divine justice.

Odysseus blinding Polyphemus. Attic grave urn found at Eleusis.

The return of the heroes. i

But in sacking Troy the Greeks committed impieties, and few of them gained an easy return. Impartial is the justice of the gods. Cassandra fled for refuge to the altar of Athena during the sack she had long foretold, that none believed, and there Locrian Ajax raped her. Ajax survived shipwreck on the voyage home and soon he was foolishly boasting to have escaped the vengeance of the gods. As he came to shore Poseidon broke the rock to which he clung and drowned him. In expiation, the Locrians send maidens to serve the shrine at Troy. The Greeks set out to exterminate the Trojan royal house; they cast Hector's son from the battlements, and sacrificed Polyxena at the tomb of Achilles. Menelaus would have slain Helen, but she bared her breast and he could not. They returned rich to Sparta by Egypt, and when they died they went to the Islands of the Blest: for Menelaus was son in law to Zeus. Neoptolemus, the son of Achilles, slew Priam at the altar of Zeus, but he avoided shipwreck on his return. Helenus advised him to go by land, taking the sorrowing Andromache, Hector's widow, and to settle where the houses had iron foundations, wooden walls and woollen roofs. In

Epirus he found the Molossians supporting their wool tents on spears, and he became their king.

The return of the heroes. ii

But he determined to recover his father's kingdom from usurpers. Late the justice of the gods overtook Neoptolemus: like Priam he died at the altar. In Delphi the priests butchered him in a quarrel over the sacrifices. Now they do him honour with a shrine. Idomeneus of Crete found a usurper in his bed. But he had vowed to sacrifice the first thing that met him on his return, and it was his daughter. Plague came on Crete and they banished him for his impiety. But some heroes stayed in Asia. Podalirius settled in Caria to be safe if the heavens fell, in a plain surrounded by high mountains. Calchas the prophet went to Colophon. There he met Mopsus, son of Apollo's bride, Tiresias's daughter, a wiser prophet than he was, and so he died. For Mopsus numbered the figs on a wild fig tree, and the pigs in the unborn farrow of a sow. A sow too marked the city for Aeneas, who escaped from Troy and came to Italy, and married the daughter of Latinus, wild son of Odysseus and Circe. Trojan Aeneas founded Rome, men of Trojan blood to take vengeance on the Greeks in later times.

The murders of Agamemnon and Clytemnestra

Agamemnon took Cassandra as his portion of the spoil, and set sail with her for Argos. But in his absence Aegisthus had seduced his wife Clytmnestra. He was Thyeste's son, and he had slain Atreus; now like his father he seduced the queen. When Agamemnon returned Clytemnestra received him with feigned joy, and made him walk on purple carpets like a god. She had small reason for joy at his homecoming; she blamed him for tricking her into sending Iphigenia as a bride to Aulis.

Then she sent him to the bath house to make ready for the feast, and there she caught him in a hunting net and struck him three blows with a double axe, sacrificing him for the prosperity of the land. She slew Cassandra too, who recognised the gory history of the house. A faithful slave smuggled out the infant Orestes, and took him to Phocis, where he came to manhood. Then he asked the oracle how he might regain his kingdom. Apollo expressed the will of Zeus, that he avenge his father on his faithless mother. He came in disguise to Argos, and cut a lock of his hair for his father's tomb. Electra his sister recognised him, though she believed him dead. Together they plotted to do the dreadful deed.

The Fate of Orestes

So Orestes slew his mother, and her paramour Aegisthus, with Electra's help. But the Furies, the old goddesses, care not for the father, and avenge the crime of blood, and haunted Orestes, driving him mad.

He fled to Apollo, who purified him with pig's blood. But the Furies were not allayed, and the ghost of Clytemnestra urged them on: for they are of the old religion. Orestes came to Athens, and there they knew the matricide, and in the feast they gave him a separate table, to avoid pollution. But not to give offence they all sat at separate tables. Then Orestes went to the Crimea, to recover the image of Artemis. Her priestess would have sacrificed him, as she did all shipwrecked Greeks. But wishing to have a message sent to Greece, she discovered her brother: for it was Iphigenia, carried off by Artemis from the sacrifice at Aulis.

She helped her brother bring the image back to Athens, and there before the Areopagus Orestes's cause was tried, and Athena gave her casting vote for acquittal: for she is born of no mother. So the Furies were appeased and the will of Zeus was seen to be accomplished.

Odysseus. i

Odysseus too returned late to find suitors devouring his house, plotting to kill his son and marry his wife Penelope and so inherit the kingdom. When he left Troy he came to Thrace, and sacked the city of the Cicones, sparing only Ismarus, priest of Apollo, who gave him a skin of finest wine, which was later to be the means of saving his life. But the Cicones rallied and drove Odysseus back to his ships. He passed the land of the Lotus Eaters, and his sailors ate the lotus and forgot their homes, and lost all longing to return. He came to the land of the Cyclops, godless one-eyed shepherds who live solitary in caves. The Cyclops Polyphemus, Poseidon's son, shut Odysseus and his men up in his cave, and each night he ate two of them raw for his supper. Odysseus made him drunk with the wine of Ismarus; this was easily done – the wine was good and very strong – and put out his eye with an olive stake. In the morning they escaped under the bellies of the Cyclops's sheep. Odysseus nearly reached home. Aeolus, king of the winds, gave him all the contrary winds tied up in a sack. In sight of Ithaca, Odysseus fell asleep, and his men, thinking it treasure, opened the sack, and the winds drove him back to Aeolus.

Odysseus. ii

They came to the land of the Laestrygons, huge giants who destroyed all the other ships with rocks. Odysseus escaped to the isle of Circe, who turned his comrades to swine. When Odysseus sought them, Hermes met him and gave him the herb moly to preserve him from enchantment. When Circe gave him the drink, he drew his sword, and forced her to free his men and swear an oath never to harm him. For one year he was her consort. She sent him to Hades to consult the soul of Tiresias: there he saw all the dead heroes and learned their fates. Then he passed the Sirens, and heard their song. For he was tied to the mast, and the rowers ears were stopped with wax. He passed between Scylla and Charybdis, steering close to Scylla and saving the ship at the cost of six men: for each of Scylla's heads siezed one. They came to the Island of the Sun: there his men slew the cattle of the Sun for food. For this sacrilege Zeus smote the ship with a thunderbolt.

Odysseus. iii

Only Odysseus escaped, clinging to the mast. Charybdis would have sucked him into her whirlpool opposite Scylla. But he clung like an octopus to a fig tree overhanging it. The waves carried him to the island of Calypso. Seven years she kept him her unwilling consort: all day he wept by the shore, but by night he entered her bed.

The gods sent Hermes who bade her release him, lest she make him immortal. He built a raft and set sail. But Poseidon saw him as he returned from feasting with the virtuous Ethiopians, and raised a storm and wrecked the raft. Ino the White Goddess saved Odysseus with her veil, and he came to the land of the Phaeacians. Nausicaa, the king's daughter, found him, waking him from sleep as she played at ball with her maidens after washing the clothes. Her mother Arete accepted him as a suppliant, but the Phaeacians despised him, until he beat them at casting the quoit. Then they gave him gifts and ferried him back to Ithaca. On their return Poseidon turned the ship to a rock, his final act of spite against Odysseus for blinding Polyphemus his son.

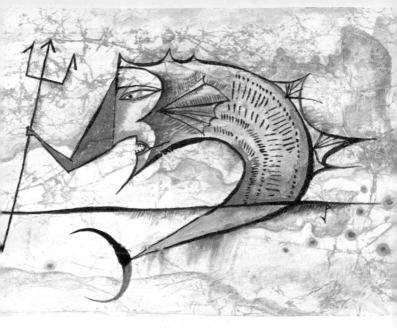

Odysseus. iv

So Odysseus returned to his kingdom. Athena guided him to the house of Eumaeus the swineherd, and made him known to Telemachus his son and they planned to overthrow the suitors. Odysseus went as a beggar to the hall: the suitors mocked him, setting him to fight the beggar Irus, whom he beat. Penelope welcomed him, ignorant of who he was: his old nurse knew him when she bathed him, by a scar.

Athena put it into Penelope's mind to set a contest for the suitors, to string the bow of Odysseus and shoot through twelve axe-rings. None could even bend the bow but Odysseus, and then Telemachus joined him with Eumaeus, and they slew all the suitors. Then he made himself known to Penelope, who proved him by the riddle of the bed, made from a growing olive tree, so that it could never be moved. He took an oar to Thesprotia, where they took it for a winnowing fan, and he begot a son on their queen and returned to Ithaca. There his other son, Telegonus son of Circe, slew him, coming from the sea to seek his father with a spear tipped with a sting ray's poisonous barb.

A dead noble mourned at his bier. Large eighth century geometric sepulchral urn from the cemetry at Athens.

The end of the heroes

Of all the heroes only Orestes was succeeded by a son, in whose reign the children of Heracles returned to claim their inheritance. The Spartans had a dual kingship, and both houses claimed descent from Heracles: so a pair of twins are said to have led one of the contingents. This genealogical fiction legitimised the new migrations into Greece, linking them to the old mythology. A number of folk tales were told about the invasion to account for the delay of a hundred years, the later division of the Peloponnese, and the reputation of each city. The mythological event corresponds to what is called the Dorian Invasion, which marks the widespread introduction to Greece of iron, of a new fashion of dressing, of cremation in place of burial and perhaps of a family structure. The 'Invasion' was not always violent and may have taken a long period of time, rather like the Anglo-Saxon invasion of England. Some places, Pylos at least, were sacked, not necessarily by the Dorians. But at the end of the process new Greeks, speakers of a different dialect associated with the North West, inhabited Boeotia and the Peloponnese, restricting the earlier Greeks to Attica and Arcadia.

The Greeks looked back on the period before the Dorians, the heroic age, as superior to their own, a note that recurs many times in the epic. This is the context of Hesiod's fable of the five ages of men, in which the age of the heroes is interposed between the Bronze men and the age of iron in which he himself was living. This was when the tensions of the small patriarchal family, possibly a Dorian introduction, turned the shame culture of the extended family into a guilt culture. The art of the Mycenaean period derived from a naturalistic technique developed in Crete. In many places it dwindled away to be replaced by a non-representational geometric style. The nobles in Athens buried the ashes of their dead in huge urns: yet they had also sophisticated ivory statuettes. This was the period when the poems of Homer were taking shape; when the myths of the Greeks were being transmitted from the period to which they apparently refer to the classical period. They provided the main subject matter of much Greek poetry and this has preserved the myths for the modern world.

The return of the sons of Heracles

The sons of Heracles returned to the Peloponnese. Eurystheus cast them out. The Athenians fought for them, and slew him, and buried his head under the road to Athens to protect the city. The Heraclids returned again, but a plague drove them out. The oracle told them to return again in the time of the third harvest. And they did, but Hyllus the son of Heracles was defeated at the isthmus. Then they knew that the oracle meant the third generation, harvest of men, and a hundred years later they crossed the Gulf of Corinth, building ships at Naupactus, and taking a three-eyed man as guide – a man riding a one-eyed horse. Then they defeated Tisamenus, son of Orestes, and took possession of the Peloponnese. They drew lots from a bucket of water, first for Argos, then for Sparta, last for Messene. Cresphontes wanted Messene, and put in a clod of earth instead of a pebble: it dissolved and the other two lots came out first. On the altars each found an omen for his city: snakes for the twin sons of Aristomachus, 'Spartans fierce in attack'; a toad 'that stays at home'; for Argive Temenus and the wily thieving fox for Cresphontes of Messene.

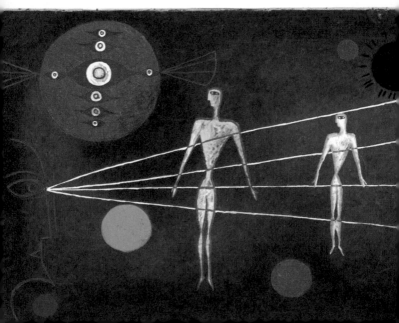

The five ages of men

Such were the fates of the heroes; some perished under seven-gated Thebes, the land of Cadmus, and some in Troy, fighting for fair-haired Helen. They were the sons of gods and mortal women, after Zeus had destroyed the race of bronze men for their impiety. For the first race of men was of gold, in the time of Cronus. They lived like gods without labour or pain, nor did they suffer from old age, but they fell asleep in death, and Earth, who bore fruit for them ungrudgingly in their life, now keeps them as givers of wealth and guardians of men.

Next came the silver race of men, inferior. They lived long as babies, a hundred years at the breast. Then in wanton violence they destroyed each other. They did not worship the gods and Zeus hid them beneath the earth. Then he made the bronze men out of ash trees, like their spears.

But all their houses and arms were bronze. They ate meat and slew one another and were destroyed in the flood. Now is the iron age. Shame and Justice have left the earth and there is no end to toil and pain.

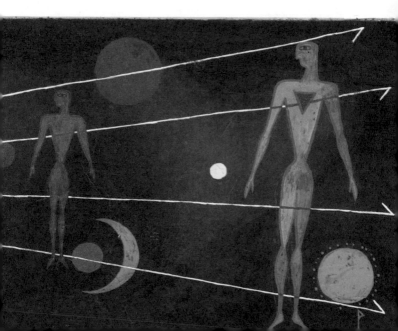

BOOKS TO READ

The Greek myths have been told and re-told at different levels and with various explanations. The volume *Greek Mythology* (from the present publisher) carries further those given briefly in this book.

The Greek Myths, Robert Graves. Penguin Books, Harmondsworth 1955 (2 vols. paperback) and Cassell, London 1958. Gives a stimulating personal view. Many reprints since the first editions.

Myths of the Greeks and Romans, Michael Grant. Weidenfeld & Nicholson, London 1962. More orthodox than Graves; has a most useful reading list.

A Handbook of Greek Mythology, H. J. Rose. Methuen, London. The 6th edition appeared in 1958; there is also a paperback. Full and scholarly.

The Gods of the Greeks, C. Kerenyi. 1951, and *The Heroes of the Greeks*, C. Kerenyi. 1959, Thames & Hudson, London. The Jungian view.

Most popular illustrated books on the Greeks – the number of which continually increases – concentrate on art and literature and idealize the Greeks. This is not true of

The Greeks, H. Lloyd-Jones. New Thinker's Library, Watts, 1962.

The Greeks, A. Andrewes. The History of Human Society. Hutchinson, London 1967.

MUSEUMS

A high proportion of Greek works of art illustrate the myths in the contemporary style of their period, especially Greek vases (where they do not depict *genre* scenes of everyday life). Sculpture is more often devoted to the idealized exploration of the male nude. The collection in the British Museum is outstanding and exceptionally well displayed. The best outside London is probably that of the Ashmolean Museum at Oxford, but most provincial museums and some universities have some Greek material. The great continental museums are beyond the scope of this note, and rival the British Museum. In North America the two finest collections are probably those of the Metropolitan Museum of Art in New York, and of the Museum of Fine Arts, Boston. But again, the major cities and universities in the east and west United States have their own collections.

In the Antipodes, the Nicholson Museum of the University of Sydney, the National Gallery of Victoria in Melbourne (with an excellent illustrated guide to the Greek vases by Professor A. D. Trendall, just published); the Otago Museum in Dunedin, and the Logie Collection in the University of Canterbury, Christchurch, all have fine collections, especially of vases.

INDEX

SOME OTHER TITLES IN THIS SERIES

 Natural History

The Animal Kingdom
Australian Animals
Bird Behaviour
Birds of Prey
Fishes of the World
Fossil Man
A Guide to the Seashore

Life in the Sea
Mammals of the World
Natural History Collecting
The Plant Kingdom
Prehistoric Animals
Snakes of the World
Wild Cats

 Gardening

Chrysanthemums
Garden Flowers

Garden Shrubs
Roses

 Popular Science

Atomic Energy
Computers at Work
Electronics

Mathematics
Microscopes & Microscopic Life
The Weather Guide

 Arts

Architecture
Jewellery

Porcelain
Victoriana

General Information

Flags
Military Uniforms
Rockets & Missiles
Sailing

Sailing Ships & Sailing Craft
Sea Fishing
Trains

 Domestic Animals & Pets

Budgerigars
Cats
Dogs

Horses & Ponies
Pets for Children

Domestic Science

Flower Arranging

 History & Mythology

Discovery of
  Africa
  The American West
  Japan
  North America

Myths & Legends of
  Ancient Egypt
  The South Seas